Study Guide for

OF CHILDREN, 4th edition, by Guy R. Lefrancois

George B. Semb

University of Kansas

Wadsworth Publishing Company
Belmont, California
A Division of Wadsworth, Inc.

Printed in the United States of America

1 2 3 4 5 6 7 8 9 10--87 86 85 84 83

ISBN 0-534-01308-2

CONTENTS

PREFACE

To the Student

This study guide is designed to help you review the material in *Of Children*, fourth edition, by Guy R. Lefrancois. It comprises a set of objectives that, if learned well, will reinforce your understanding of the topics covered in the text.

Each chapter of the study guide opens with an introduction to the subject matter followed by a list of key terms and concepts and a series of associated short-answer essay questions. It concludes with a posttest.

I recommend that you begin your study by scanning the entire chapter, noting main headings and carefully reading the entire assignment. Next, define the key terms and concepts and respond to the short-answer questions in your own words. If a concept or question is confusing, or if you do not fully understand it, reread the appropriate section of the text. If you then find yourself copying a response directly from the text, it probably means that your understanding of the concept is still unclear. In that case you should discuss the material with another student or the instructor.

Some of you may be wondering why this study guide emphasizes definitions and short essays--why it does not simply outline the main points in each chapter. From everything that is currently known about learning, active participation is an important variable in the learning process. Unlike an outline, which represents a passive approach, this study guide encourages your active participation through the written responses.

The posttest consists of multiple-choice questions. Some chapters also contain crossword puzzles to further reinforce the key terms and concepts. After you complete the posttest exercises, check your answers against those provided at the end of the chapter.

I hope the study guide helps you learn the material in *Of Children* effectively and enjoyably. If it succeeds, it has served a useful purpose.

Instructions for Answering Multiple-Choice Questions

The multiple-choice posttest is designed to reinforce what you have learned in each chapter. To help you get the greatest benefit from these questions, however, you should know several things about their construction.

First, each item has only <u>one</u> answer; that is, you will never have to select more than one alternative. Second, several questions have an alternative that reads, "all of the above," or, "all of the above are correct," or, "both (a) and (b) are correct." As a suggested procedure for answering these items, read each alternative carefully. If more than one is correct, select the most comprehensive response. For example, consider the following items:

1. Topeka is: (a) a state capital; (b) located in Kansas; (c) a city with a population of over 20,000; (d) all of the above.

Since alternatives (a), (b), and (c) are all correct, (d) is the best answer.

2. Which of the following statements is correct? (a) What a child becomes is a function of both heredity and the environment. (b) The concept of an "average child" is a useful tool for psychologists. (c) Both (a) and (b) are correct. (d) Neither (a) nor (b) is correct.

Since both (a) and (b) are accurate statements, (c) is the best alternative.

3. Which of the following statements is correct? (a) Jean Piaget was the father of psychoanalytic theory. (b) B.F. Skinner invented the first test of intelligence. (c) Both (a) and (b) are correct. (d) Neither (a) nor (b) is correct.

Since both (a) and (b) are inaccurate statements, (d) is the best alternative.

4. Which of the following statements is correct? (a) Most children utter their first meaningful word by the time they are three months old. (b) A child's most dramatic motor development during infancy is learning to walk. (c) Depth perception does not develop until the child is approximately two years old. (d) All of the above are correct.

In this example, alternatives (a) and (c) are enticing but only (b) is an accurate statement.

To the Instructor

Of Children and this study guide lend themselves equally well to lecture classes, individualized instruction, modular scheduling, computer-aided instruction, Keller and Sherman's Personalized System of Instruction (PSI), and small group discussions. The study guide is suitable for students who need step-by-step instruction or who simply wish to review the material quickly. Its aim is to help students learn the material you assign.

The structure of each chapter is based on the mastery concept. The sections Key Terms and Concepts and Short-Answer Questions actively involve the student in the learning process. Questions in the Test Item File for Of Children build on the material outlined in the study guide. In addition, I have constructed several questions for each key term and concept to permit repeated testing and have devised a number of challenging exercises that require students to analyze, evaluate, integrate, and apply the material they have learned.

If you have any questions about the use of these materials in your course--whether your instructional format is lecture, individualized, computer-aided, PSI, or small group discussion, please write to me at the Department of Human Development, University of Kansas, Lawrence, Kansas 66045 or call me at (913) 864-4840.

Field-Testing Procedures

All of the material in this study guide has been intensively field-tested by experienced undergraduates, whose comments about design, content, and organization have been integrated into each chapter. The field test team also made a detailed analysis of the multiple-choice items in the posttest. I used the same procedure in preparing the Test Item File for Of Children.

Acknowledgments

Several individuals helped prepare, revise, and field-test this study guide. I am particularly grateful to John Drake for his invaluable feedback, criticism, and encouragement, and to Angela Calef and Mary Helen Velasquez-Drake for their superb secretarial and editing skills.

About the Author

George B. Semb is a professor of human development at the University of Kansas. He has written study guides for texts in introductory psychology, aviation, behavior analysis, and introductory biology. His primary area of interest is analyzing instructional systems, in particular, Keller and Sherman's Personalized System of Instruction (PSI). He has used PSI in his own courses for twelve years and has written several articles dealing with PSI and other forms of individualized instruction. Many of the techniques he has investigated are incorporated in this study guide.

CHAPTER 1:

THE BEGINNING

Introduction

Development can be viewed from the perspective of the evolution of the human race--of changes that occurred over a period of 4.5 billion years. It can also be viewed from the perspective of changes in a single individual in the course of one lifetime. In many ways, the changes that define <u>ontogeny</u> (the development of a single individual) are no less dramatic than those that define <u>phylogeny</u> (the development of the species). The resemblance between a single fertilized egg--one microscopic speck--and an adult human is surely no greater than that between creatures that roamed the swamps of this planet 500 million years ago and those now beginning to understand the process of evolution.

Child development is concerned primarily with the growth and development of single individuals (ontogeny). It is useful, nevertheless, to be aware of the parallels between phylogeny and ontogeny, for they suggest questions and answers for the study of children. The most obvious, and perhaps the most important, of these questions concerns adaptation. Presumably adaptation allowed some species to survive; failure to adapt meant extinction for others. Is it not true that an individual child's development is characterized by his or her adaptation to a world that becomes more complex as he or she becomes more aware of it? And, do not children themselves become more complex as they learn to deal with the world more effectively? What are the mechanisms that allow children to change and adapt? These are the questions underlying the study of child development. Child development is a recent science; some of its methods and answers, which are still unfolding, are introduced in the first chapter.

Key Terms and Concepts

1. Phylogenetic vs. ontogenetic development
    Epigenesis

2. Developmental psychology
    Major tasks of developmental psychologists
    Recurring themes
    Heredity vs. environment

1

       Active vs. passive processes
       Continuous process vs. distinct stages

3. Major developmental processes
      Growth, maturation, and learning
      Development vs. learning

4. History of child development
      Infant mortality
      Hospitalism
      Locke and Rousseau
      Early child psychologists
        G. Stanley Hall
        Alfred Binet
        John B. Watson
        Sigmund Freud

5. Methods of studying children
      Naturalistic observations
        Diary description
        Specimen description
        Time sampling
        Event sampling
      Correlational studies--correlation vs. causation
      Experiments
        Independent variable
        Dependent variable
        Experimental group
        Control group
      Longitudinal and cross-sectional research
        Longitudinal studies
        Cross-sectional studies
        Combined approaches

6. Problems in psychological research
      Generalizability
      Sampling
      Ecological validity
      Memory
      Honesty
      Experimenter bias--double blind procedure
      Subject bias

7. Children's rights
      Recent court rulings
      Informed consent

8. The average child

Short-Answer Questions

1. Phylogeny vs. ontogeny

    a. Distinguish between phylogenetic and ontogenetic development.
        Give an example of each.

    b. State two ways in which ontogeny and phylogeny are related.

    c. Define epigenesis.

    d. Interaction between what two major factors determines the
        development of a child into an adult?

2. Developmental psychology

    a. Define the term development.

    b. Name the three major tasks facing developmental psy-
        chologists.

c. Identify three recurring issues in child psychology that still remain largely unresolved. (Remember: The issues themselves illustrate that how we study children is strongly influenced by the assumptions we make.)

3. Developmental processes

    a. Define and give an example of each of the following: growth; maturation; learning.

    b. What is the central difference between learning and development? How does this difference contribute to the questions learning theorists and developmental theorists typically ask?

4. History of child development

    a. Give two reasons why the scientific study of children is such a recent endeavor.

    b. Identify at least two factors contributing to high infant mortality rates during the past two centuries.

    c. Define hospitalism.

d. How did Locke and Rousseau differ in their views of children?

e. Briefly describe the contribution to child psychology made by each of the following: G. Stanley Hall; Alfred Binet; John B. Watson; Sigmund Freud.

5. Methods of studying children

a. Define naturalistic observation and give an example of the following techniques: diary description; specimen description; time sampling; event sampling.

b. Briefly describe what is meant by a correlational study.

c. What is the difference between correlation and causation? Which is necessary for the other?

d. State under what circumstances a correlational study might be more desirable than an experiment.

e. Explain the difference between <u>independent</u> and <u>dependent</u> <u>variables</u>. Design a simple experiment illustrating this difference. (Do not use one from the text.)

f. Define the terms <u>experimental</u> and <u>control</u> <u>groups</u>. Explain why control groups are used.

g. Identify the dependent and independent variables in the Ypsilanti Project. State how the experimental and control groups differed before and after the experiment. Explain how this difference is related to the independent variable.

h. Define and give an example of <u>longitudinal</u> research. Cite at least one major limitation of <u>this type of study</u>.

i. Define and give an example of <u>cross-sectional</u> research. Cite at least one major limitation of this type of study, and name at least one advantage it has over longitudinal research.

j. Define and give an example of a longitudinal/cross-sectional study and state how it overcomes the disadvantages of each of the separate methods it uses.

6. Problems in psychological research

   a. According to Lefrancois, what is the single most important criterion for evaluating psychological research? Briefly explain why.

   b. Explain how sampling is related to the generalizability of psychological research.

   c. Define and give an example of ecological validity.

   d. State why cultural variables are important in interpreting the results of psychological studies.

   e. Briefly describe how memory and honesty can affect psychological research.

f. To what does the term <u>experimenter</u> <u>bias</u> refer? Give an example and describe one way to guard against this type of bias.

g. What is subject bias? Give an example.

7. <u>Children's rights</u>

a. Briefly describe the current trend in recent court decisions pertaining to the rights of children.

b. Define <u>informed</u> <u>consent</u> and state why it is now a common practice among child researchers.

8. <u>The average child</u>

a. What is the average child?

b. Of what use is this concept to psychologists?

1. Phylogeny refers to: (a) the combined effects of maturation, growth, and learning; (b) the development of individuals within a species; (c) the development of a species; (d) the study of child behavior and development.

2. Developmental psychology is concerned primarily with: (a) an anaysis of individuals within a species; (b) the analysis of species; (c) the relationship between ontogenetic and phylogenetic learning; (d) those aspects of human behavior that change from childhood to adulthood.

3. Maturation may be defined as changes that: (a) are dependent primarily upon the child's environment; (b) are frequently attributed to genetic predispositions; (c) are primarily quantitative; (d) none of the above.

4. Which of the following statements is correct? (a) Developmental psychology is more concerned with discovering the underlying principles of learning than with describing differences between the learning processes of children and adults; (b) Hospitalism, a common disorder among children in the 1800s and 1900s, refers to the child's fear of hospitals and children's homes; (c) The scientific study of children is among the oldest of the social sciences; (d) None of the above is correct.

5. (   ) described children as active and enquiring; their minds develop through deliberate and purposeful interaction with the environment: (a) Binet; (b) Hall; (c) Locke; (d) Rousseau.

6. (   ) emphasized the importance of the child's early years on subsequent personality development: (a) Alfred Binet; (b) Sigmund Freud; (c) G. Stanley Hall; (d) John B. Watson.

7. Which of the following is not a common naturalistic technique for observing children: (a) diary description; (b) direct experimentation; (c) event sampling; (d) time sampling.

8. Which of the following statements is correct? (a) If two variables are sufficiently correlated, one must cause the other; (b) If two variables are sufficiently correlated, one must necessarily follow from the other; (c) No matter how high the correlation between two variables, we cannot infer that one causes the other; (d) All of the above are correct, since they all say the same thing.

9. Suppose a researcher compares the college grade point averages of sixty students randomly selected from high-income families to the grade point averages of sixty students randomly selected from low-income families. Further, suppose the researcher finds that students from low-income families have higher grade point averages than students from high-income families. One conclusion that can legitimately be drawn from this study is that: (a) students from low-income families are highly motivated to perform well because that will increase their chances of getting a good job; (b) there is a causal connection between family income level and grade point average in college; (c) both (a) and (b) are legitimate conlusions; (d) neither (a) nor (b) is a legitimate conclusion.

10. In an experiment designed to determine whether sixth-grade middle-class girls perform better than sixth-grade middle-class boys on tests of language ability, the dependent variable is each child's: (a) grade level in school; (b) language performance; (c) sex; (d) social class.

11. Suppose a researcher randomly assigns fifty sixth-grade students to one of two groups (A and B). Group A receives praise from the teacher for correctly solving math problems while Group B does not. The researcher then measures the number of math problems each group does. The independent variable in this study is: (a) the number of math problems each group does; (b) the praise from the teacher; (c) the random assignment of students to groups; (d) the use of an experiment rather than a survey.

12. In a well-designed experiment, the control group should be: (a) as different from the experimental group as possible before the experiment begins; (b) equivalent to the experimental group after the experiment ends; (c) equivalent to the experimental group before the experiment begins; (d) none of the above.

13. A study that involves comparing the behavior of a child at one age to the same child's behavior at a different age defines a/an ( ) study: (a) cross-sectional; (b) experimental; (c) longitudinal; (d) ontogenic.

14. To determine whether the average eight-year-old is more intelligent than the average four-year-old, the most practical and economical approach would be a/an ( ) study: (a) cross-sectional; (b) experimental; (c) longitudinal; (d) time sampling.

15. According to Lefrancois, the single most important criterion for evaluating psychological research is: (a) generalizability; (b) honesty; (c) interpretation; (d) the experimenter's bias.

16. Suppose you have two randomly selected groups of 18-year-old college males. One group is decidedly overweight and the other is not. Next, suppose a psychologist who believes that weight is an important factor in adjusting to college, interviews all of the students to discover who is "normally adjusted." She finds that a higher proportion of the overweights are maladjusted. Before you accept the results of her study, which of the following potential sources of error should you question most closely: (a) biased sampling; (b) experimenter bias; (c) memory distortion; (d) subject bias.

17. Researchers use a double-blind procedure primarily to guard against: (a) experimenter bias; (b) sampling error; (c) subject dishonesty; (d) the imperfect memories of subjects who participate in their research.

18. One reason why some experimental preschool programs may be successful is that children and their parents are aware that they are part of a special program. This is an example of: (a) a double-blind procedure; (b) a sampling error; (c) experimenter bias; (d) subject bias.

19. The overriding theme of recent court decisions on children's rights is that laws concerning children, and their application, must: (a) guarantee that children are capable of making all decisions with respect to their own welfare; (b) protect the rights of children rather than the rights of their parents; (c) provide for the informed consent of both the parent and the child before the child is allowed to participate in a research study; (d) all of the above.

20. The average child: (a) does not exist; (b) is a useful conceptual tool for psychologists; (c) both (a) and (b) ; (d) neither (a) nor (b) .

Answers to Posttest

1. c (p. 2) 2. d (p. 3) 3. b (p. 4) 4. d (p. 5) 5. d (p. 8)
6. b (p. 9) 7. b (p. 10) 8. c (p. 11) 9. d (p. 11) 10. b (p. 12)
11. b (p. 12) 12. c (p. 12) 13. c (p. 13) 14. a (p. 13) 15. a (p. 15)
16. b (p. 17) 17. a (p. 17) 18. d (p. 18) 19. b (p. 18) 20. c (p. 20)

CHAPTER 2:

HEREDITY AND ENVIRONMENT

Introduction

It is generally accepted that human development depends on both heredity and environment, yet there is considerable controversy concerning the relative importance of each factor. In the late nineteenth century, Galton observed that most of Britain's better scientists came from a small number of families. He then concluded that genius, and all other personality characteristics, are inherited, and he advocated that people, like domestic animals, should be selectively bred. Watson, on the other hand, reasoned that since whatever a person becomes is a function of learning, the environment must be responsible for genius and other human qualities. The heredity-environment controversy has continued ever since. Recently, Jensen gave added impetus to the question by publishing a hypothesis that tends to support Galton's original conclusion.

The first part of Chapter 2 examines the biological process of heredity, discussing in turn, ova, sperm, cells, chromosomes, genes, DNA, molecules, chromosomal abnormalities, cloning, and eugenics. A great deal is known about the mechanisms of heredity; much still remains a mystery. However, we are considerably closer to the remediation of genetic abnormalities than we were a few years ago. How close we are remains to be seen, and related ethical and moral questions remain to be answered.

The second part of the chapter examines the heredity-environment issue. Several studies are cited to support the belief that heredity is most important in determining development. The evidence includes studies of families (the Jukes and the Kallikaks), of animals (most notably, Tryon's success in breeding maze-bright and maze-dull rats), and of twins. Genetic contributions to schizophrenia and intelligence are also discussed.

Even if we accept the idea that heredity sets certain limits for intellectual development and makes some personality characteristics more probable than others, we must admit that environment is largely responsible for permitting or preventing the manifestation of these predispositions. Even some genetically determined physiological defects can be dramatically influenced by an environmental factor as simple as diet. Because we have some control over the environment and very little over heredity, the psychologist's greatest emphasis should probably be on the environment rather than on heredity. This chapter

12

reviews some of the studies that have most dramatically illustrated the potentially beneficial effects of an enriched environment, particularly for individuals from deprived backgrounds. They involve experiments in which the brains of rats were actually modified physically, presumably as a result of their environment, and studies where mental retardation in orphans was dramatically arrested following significant environmental changes.

The studies reviewed in this chapter make it clear that environment can affect development beneficially. It follows, as well, that deprived environments can produce an opposite effect, although, as Kagan has found, such effects are not irreversible. Finally, it should be noted that the environment will have its most pronounced effect on a trait during the period of most rapid growth, hence, the tremendous importance of a child's very early environment.

The chapter ends with an analysis of two hypotheses concerning the relative contribution of heredity and environment to intelligence--Jensen's heritability hypothesis, and the Stern "rubber-band" hypothesis. The debate is not resolved. The important question is not whether heredity and environment affect different aspects of development, but <u>how</u> and <u>when</u>.

<u>Key</u> <u>Terms</u> <u>and</u> <u>Concepts</u>

1. Wild (feral) children: two hypotheses

2. Mechanisms of heredity
   Conception: ovum + sperm = zygote
   Mitosis and meiosis
   Chromosomes: autosomes and sex chromosomes
   Sex chromosomes: XX and XY
   Genes: recessive and dominant
   DNA

3. Genetic abnormalities
   Sickle cell anemia
   Mongolism: Down's syndrome
   Turner's syndrome (XO)
   Klinefelter's syndrome (XXY)
   XYY syndrome
   Amniocentesis

4. Phenotypes, genotypes, and canalization
   Genotype
   Phenotype
   Canalization
   Epigenesis

5. Environment or heredity?

13

6. Family studies
    Francis Galton's observations
    Eugenics
    Frederick the Great and Alfred Noyes
    The Jukes and the Kallikaks

7. Animal studies
    Tryon's selective breeding of rats
    Kreck's environmental manipulation of rats

8. Studies of deprived children
    Sherman and Keys' study of the Hollow Children
        Common gene pool
        Independent and dependent variables
        Main findings

9. Institutionalized children
    The Dennis study of orphanages in Iran
    Lee's study of changes in intelligence test scores
    Absolute vs. relative retardation (Kagan)

10. Twins
    Fraternal (dyzygotic) vs. identical (monozygotic) twins
    Intrauterine vs. postnatal environment
    Genetic relatedness and intelligence test scores
    Identical twins reared together vs. those reared apart
    Schizophrenia may have a genetic base

11. The Jensen hypothesis
    Burt's data
    Jensen's hypothesis
    Major criticisms

12. Stern's "rubber-band" hypothesis

13. The issue: <u>how</u> heredity and the environment contribute.

Short-Answer Questions

1. <u>Wild children</u>

    a. Why do psychologists study <u>wild</u> (feral) children?

b. A hypothesis is a possible explanation for some phenomenon. What are the two alternative hypotheses that might account for retarded behavior among wild children?

c. Explain how these hypotheses contradict each other.

2. Mechanisms of heredity

a. Conception marks the beginning of life with the physical union of two cells. Name the two cells and their sources. How do each of these cells compare in size?

b. What is a zygote?

c. What is a chromosome? What does it carry?

d. Briefly describe the two types of cell division: mitosis and meiosis. Be sure to indicate how many chromosomes are present at the beginning and at the end of each process.

e. What is an autosome?

f. Who determines the sex of offspring? Why?

g. How many chromosomes does a zygote contain? Explain how it
    gets this particular compliment.

h. Genes are the smallest units of heredity. How many does the
    typical cell contain?

i. Define the terms recessiveness and dominance.

j. Suppose two genes (pink and blue) determine eye color.   What
    are the three possible combinations of pink and blue genes?
    If pink is dominant, indicate the genetic outcome for each
    combination.

k. What is DNA?

3. Genetic abnormalities

    a. What is sickle cell anemia? Briefly describe its effects and
        whom it typically afflicts.

    b. Match each statement, description, or symptom with its ap-
        propriate syndrome.   (Each statement has only one correct
        syndrome.)

Syndromes

1. Down's syndrome
2. Turner's (XO)
3. Klinefelter's (XXY)
4. XYY

Statements, descriptions, and symptoms

___produces "super" males
___affects only females
___most common chromosomal birth defect
___occurs more often with older mothers
___produces tall and muscular individuals
___produces underdeveloped secondary sex characteristics
___produces both male and female secondary sex characteristics
___affected individuals have a higher incidence of criminal
   behavior
   than similarly appearing individuals in the general population
___individuals with this syndrome were once sent to the Olympics
   to
   compete as females

c. What is amniocentesis? Why is it used? What are the risks
   involved?

4. Phenotypes, genotypes, and canalization

   a. Define phenotype.

   b. Define genotype.

   c. Define canalization. Give an example of a highly canalized
      characteristic and one not highly canalized.

d. Of what relevance is canalization to evolutionary theory?

e. Define <u>epigenesis</u>.

5. <u>Environment</u> <u>or</u> <u>heredity</u>: the nature-nurture controversy

6. <u>Family</u> <u>studies</u>

a. Define <u>eugenics</u>. Give an example.

b. Galton observed that most of England's outstanding men were
    either related to or came from a small number of families.
    What did this observation lead him to conclude about the
    sources of intelligence?

c. Briefly describe the attempts of Frederick the Great and
    Alfred Noyes to practice eugenics.

d. Goddard's study of the Jukes and the Kallikaks is often cited
    as evidence that intelligence is largely determined by
    heredity. How might the results of this study support an en-
    vironmental interpretation? Explain.

e. Identify three grounds on which the study of the Kallikaks has been criticized.

7. Animal studies

    a. In the Tryon experiment on the inheritance of learning ability in rats, how were the bright and dull groups initially determined?

    b. What was the dependent variable in Tryon's experiment?

    c. What rats were eliminated as each generation produced its offspring? Why? How many successive generations of rats were involved?

    d. Why were offspring from dull parents occasionally exchanged with those from bright parents? Had Tryon not made these exchanges, how would the results of the study been affected? Explain.

    e. What were the results of the Tryon study? That is, what was the relationship between the brightest of the dull rats and the dullest of the bright rats at the end of the experiment?

f. In Krech's experiment with rats and intelligence, how did the treatment of the two groups differ? That is, what was the independent variable? Be specific.

g. How did the rats in Krech's two groups differ with respect to how quickly they solved the maze problem?

h. What do Krech's findings suggest about the contribution of the environment to intelligence? Explain.

8. Sherman and Key's study of the Hollow Children

a. Supposedly, the Hollow Children shared a common gene pool. Explain why this assumption is an important one.

b. What was the independent variable in the study? Explain how it was defined.

c. What was the dependent variable? That is, what did Sherman and Key measure?

d. Explain why Briarsville was also included in the study.

e. Briefly describe the two main findings of the study.

9. Institutionalized children

    a. Name some of the independent variables in the Dennis study of
        institutionalized children in Iran. That is, what differen-
        tiated Institutions I and II from Institution III?

    b. Name three of the dependent variables (see text, Table 2.2).

    c. According to the text, there was only one Institution I. Why
        is Institution I listed twice in Table 2.2? Does Institution
        III have an age group comparable to that in Institution II?
        Explain.

    d. What percentage of the 2.00-2.99-year-old group in Institu-
        tion I could walk holding with support? How many children
        does this actually represent?

    e. Does walking alone decrease, increase, or stay the same with
        increased age in Institutions I and II? That is, what is the
        relationship between walking alone and age?

f. What do the overall results of the Dennis study suggest about the role of early experience in child development? Explain.

g. What do the results of Lee's study of black children in Philadelphia suggest in terms of when the children moved from the South to Philadelphia? What do they suggest about the changes in IQ scores for the children who had moved at a young age?

h. What is the difference between absolute and relative retardation? Briefly explain how Kagan's study of Guatemalan children relates to this distinction.

10. Twins

Sometimes the distinction between fraternal and identical twins is difficult to grasp. Exercises a-f may help clarify the terms.

a. The technical term for a fertilized egg is _____.
b. Identical twins come from the same fertilized egg, thus they are called _____.
c. Fraternal twins come from different fertilized eggs, thus they are called _____.
d. T F Dyzygotic twins share the same prenatal or intrauterine environment.
e. T F Monozygotic twins are genetically identical.
f. Think for a minute. Name one way in which fraternal twins are similar to ordinary siblings. Think for another minute. Name two ways fraternal twins are different from ordinary siblings.

g. Studies of twins are frequently cited in the nature-nurture controversy. What is the correlation between monozygotic twins on intelligence test scores? Is it higher or lower than the correlation for dyzygotic twins? What does this suggest about the relationship between heredity and intelligence? Explain.

h. The correlation between fraternal twins on intelligence test scores is higher than that for other siblings. What does this suggest about the influence of environment on intelligence? Explain your answer.

i. Study test Figure 2.9. Describe in your own words the relationship between genetic similarity and correlations on intelligence test scores. Next, describe the relationship between being reared together versus being reared apart. What does the latter relationship suggest about the heredity-environment issue?

j. There are greater similarities between identical twins than between fraternal twins as measured by correlations on intelligence test scores. Some psychologists argue that this supports heredity as a critical factor in determining intelligence. If you were an environmentalist, how might you interpret these data? Explain.

k. In the Newman, Freeman, and Holzinger study, identify the in-
    dependent variable (be precise), and name three dependent
    variables the authors measured. Does the high correlation
    between both groups of twins with respect to height support
    nature or nurture? Explain.

l. Schizophrenia is a psychological disorder. Briefly describe
    the evidence indicating that schizophrenia may have a genetic
    component.

11. The Jensen hypothesis

a. On what grounds have Sir Cyril Burt's data been questioned?

b. Briefly describe how Jensen arrived at the conclusion that
    only about 20 percent of the variation in intelligence test
    scores is due to environmental factors.

c. What is Jensen's hypothesis concerning racial differences in
    measured intelligence?

d. Cite at least four criticisms of Jensen's hypothesis.

12. Stern's "rubber-band" hypothesis

    a. Explain Stern's hypothesis in your own words.

    b. Give an example illustrating Stern's hypothesis.

    c. What is the basic issue in that nature-nurture controversy? Explain.

Multiple-Choice Posttest

1. One reason wild (feral) children may appear retarded is that they lack human contact during their formative years. This explanation for apparent mental retardation among such children: (a) has been proven by recent research to be accurate; (b) is referred to as an hypothesis; (c) would more likely be held by someone who sided with the heredity side of the heredity-environment controversy; (d) all of the above.

2. Which of the following statements is correct? (a) Males produce sperm cells approximately once every two to three days; (b) On the average, women produce a new ovum once every 28 minutes; (c) Sperm cells have long tails which help them to swim; (d) The ovum is the smallest cell in the human body.

3. Who determines the sex of the offspring? (a) the female, since she has XY chromosomes; (b) the female, since she has XX chromosomes; (c) the male, since he has XY chromosomes; (d) the male, since he has YY chromosomes.

4. Genes: (a) are located on chromosome; (b) are the actual units of heredity; (c) number in the thousands; (d) are all of the above.

5. A recessive gene: (a) contains less DNA than a dominant gene; (b) is a chainlike molecule consisting of different sequences of four chemical subunits; (c) will determine a hereditary trait only if combined with another recessive gene; (d) is all of the above.

6. (   ) syndrome affects females and is characterized by the absence of one number of the XX pair (thus, they are called XO). If they survive, they typically do not develop secondary sexual characteristics unless treated with hormones at an early age: (a) Down's; (b) Klinefelter's; (c) The Supermale; (d) Turner's.

7. Amniocentesis is a procedure used to: (a) destroy chromosomal aberrations; (b) fertilize the ovum in utero; (c) obtain a sample of the fluid surrounding the unborn fetus in utero; (d) select individuals to mate.

8. Which of the following statements is correct? (a) Amniocentesis is a procedure used to implement a fertilized egg in the uterine wall; (b) Epigenesis refers to the unfolding of genetically determined aspects of development; (c) The correspondence between phenotype and genotype increases as the degree of canalization decreases; (d) All of the above are correct.

9. Frederick the Great's attempts to mate tall and strong soldiers with robust peasant girls is an example of which of the following: (a) amniocentesis; (b) cloning; (c) epigenesis; (d) eugenics.

10. In Tryon's study of bright and dull rats: (a) dull rats produced by bright parents and bright rats produced by dull parents were eliminated from the study to accentuate the difference between groups; (b) the groups were initially determined by randomly assigning rats to either the bright or dull group; (c) with successive generations, the two groups became more and more similar; (d) all of the above.

11. The results of selective breeding experiments such as Tryon's suggest that: (a) activity levels of selectively bred mice remain remarkably stable over successive generations; (b) behavioral traits such as aggressiveness and emotionality can be modified by selective breeding; (c) some aspects of learning ability can be inherited; (d) all of the above.

12. On the basis of Tryon's and Krech's studies of maze-learning ability in rats, what conclusions can be drawn? (a) If you wanted to produce a group of maze-bright animals as quickly as possible, it would probably be more expedient to concentrate on the environment; (b) Maze ability is probably a result of both genetic and environmental factors; (c) Both (a) and (b) are legitimate conclusions; (d) Neither (a) or (b) is a legitimate conclusion.

13. The dependent variable in the Sherman and Key (1932) study of the Hollow Children was: (a) performance on intelligence tests; (b) the degree of genetic similarity between the respective hollows; (c) the distance the children lived from civilization; (d) none of the above.

14. In the Sherman and Key study (1932) of the Hollow Children: (a) children in all hollows performed equally well on intelligence tests due to their similar genetic background but showed marked differences on tests of aptitude and motivation due to different environments; (b) isolation of each hollow was defined in terms of the distance from the "outside" world and amount of environmental impoverishment; (c) there was striking evidence that initially retarded children in the inner hollows became less retarded as they got older; (d) all of the above.

15. The most significant finding of Lee's study of black children was that: (a) those who moved to Philadelphia at an early age or who were born there performed better than those who had moved there later; (b) those who moved to Philadelphia at an early age or were born there performed the same as those who moved there at a later age; (c) those who moved to Philadelphia later performed better than those who were born there or who had moved there at an early age; (d) younger children performed less well than older children.

16. Which of the following statements is correct? (a) Dyzygotic twins are no more alike genetically than ordinary siblings; (b) Greater similarity between monozygotic twins relative to dyzygotic twins reflect the effects of the environment; (c) Monozygotic (identical) twins share the same uterine environment (womb) while dyzygotic (fraternal) twins do not; (d) All of the above are correct.

17. Correlations of sets of intelligence test scores are generally highest among pairs of: (a) dyzygotic (fraternal) twins; (b) monozygotic (identical) twins; (c) parent-child; (d) siblings.

18. If two twins have the same IQ scores, it follows that they MUST:
(a) be identical; (b) have been raised together; (c) both
(a) and (b) ; (d) neither (a) nor (b) .

19. Kagan's study of primitive Guatemalan children suggests that
retardation: (a) caused by a deprived environment can be
reversed; (b) is relative since it continues to be evident for
many years after exposure to a deprived environment; (c) both
(a) and (b) ; (d) neither (a) nor (b) .

20. Jensen contends that about (   ) of the variation among groups
in intelligence test scores is due to genetic factors and that
(   ) is accounted for by the environment: (a) 20%; 80%;
(b) 40%; 60%; (c) 60%; 40%; (d) 80%; 20%.

21. Jensen's hypothesis: (a) is based on the intuitive theory that
genetics and the environment each contribute equally to intelligence; (b) is just that, a hypothesis; it cannot be proven or
disproven; (c) states that since we can do relatively little
about genetic influences, we should concentrate on environmental
influences; (d) all of the above.

22. Jensen's hypothesis has been criticized on the grounds that:
(a) other factors, such as nutrition, were not controlled;
(b) since there is so much overlap among gene pools, the concept
of "race" is no longer valid; (c) there is no evidence that the
heritability of intelligence is the same in all races; (d) all
of the above.

23. Stern's rubber band hypothesis contends that: (a) approximately
80% of the variance in intelligence test scores is due to
heredity; (b) heredity is more elastic than the environment;
(c) measures of intelligence are invalid because they have no
elasticity; (d) what happens to a person's genetic endowment is
a result of outside environmental influences.

24. Which of the following statements represents the most logical
resolution of the nature-nurture controversy? (a) Environment is
most important, but only for individuals who have a normal or
above normal genetic compliment; (b) Heredity and environment
interact to influence development; (c) Heredity is more important, but environmental factors can help remedy behavioral
deficits; (d) The environment is like a rubber band that
stretches to meet the needs of the child's genetic endowment.

1. b (p. 24) 2. c (p. 26) 3. c (p. 27) 4. d (p. 29) 5. c (p. 29)
6. d (p. 31) 7. c (p. 34) 8. a (p. 35) 9. d (p. 36) 10. a (p. 37)
11. d (p. 38) 12. c (p. 38) 13. a (p. 41) 14. b (p. 41) 15. a (p. 46)
16. a (p. 45) 17. b (p. 50) 18. d (p. 51) 19. a (p. 44) 20. d (p. 53)
21. b (p. 53) 22. d (p. 53) 23. d (p. 55) 24. b (p. 56)

Crossword Puzzle

Across

3. Technical term for twins who originate from different eggs
6. Type of rat who is slow to solve a maze problem
7. Ma and __ Kettle
10. Proposed the "rubber-band" hypothesis
11. Technical term for identical twins
13. An indefinite article
14. A young boy is frequently referred to as one of these
16. Parents should provide a lot of this for their children
17. Abbreviation for deoxyribonucleic acid
18. The sound a glass makes when tapped with a spoon
20. The smallest unit of heredity
21. Sex cell constituent
24. Another name for mongolism
26. Controversial psychologist who argues that the environment's contribution to intelligence is minimal
27. Psychologist who successfully bred bright and dull rats
28. A form of genetic engineering in which specific individuals are selected for reproduction
30. Technical term for a female sex cell
32. Common word for the largest cell in the human female body
33. A procedure for sampling the fluid that surrounds the unborn fetus
34. A psychological disorder that may have a significant genetic component
35. A child uses this to hear things

Down

1. What an IQ test supposedly measures
2. Three _____ mice
4. A freshly fertilized egg
5. A child would look in one to find cows, horses, and chickens
6. Type of gene which determines specific genetic outcome
7. Gregor Mendel looked in a pod to find one of these

8. A possible explanation for some event or phenomenon
9. Another name for feral children
10. _____ cell anemia
12. Soup sometimes comes in one of these
15. Infants in the U.S. are likely to call their fathers by this name
19. A syndrome characterized by the presence of both male and female secondary sex characteristics
22. A male sex cell
23. When a parent cell divides into two identical "daughters"
25. Organ in the female where eggs are stored
27. A syndrome describing children born with a missing sex chromosome
29. A type of dancer; the first one performed in San Francisco
31. Prefix meaning single

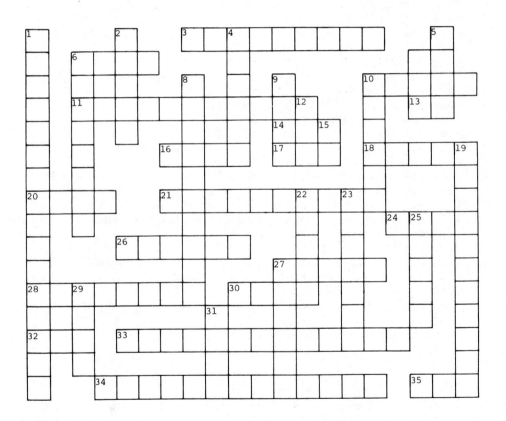

<u>Solution</u> <u>to</u> <u>Crossword</u> <u>Puzzle</u>

<u>Across</u>

3. dyzygotic
6. dull
7. Pa
10. Stern
11. monozygotic
13. an
14. lad
16. love
17. DNA
18. klink
20. gene
21. chromosome
24. Down
26. Jensen
27. Tryon
28. eugenics
30. ovum
32. egg
33. amniocentesis
34. schizophrenia
35. ear

<u>Down</u>

1. intelligence test
2. blind
4. zygote
5. barn
6. dominant
7. pea
8. hypothesis
9. wild
10. sickle
12. can
15. Da
19. Klinefelter
22. sperm
23. mitosis
25. ovary
27. Turner
29. go-go
31. mono

CHAPTER 3:

THEORIES OF CHILD DEVELOPMENT

Introduction

Psychologists have different ways of looking at children or adults. They can be concerned with their personalities, their minds, or with their behavior in social situations. Furthermore, psychologists bring different orientations to their study of human beings, and these orientations affect their observations, the questions they ask, and the answers they allegedly discover. Chapter 3 presents several theories of development. They are different because the theorists responsible for their formulation had different orientations and because they were interested in different aspects of child development.

The first is a stage theory. It was advanced by Sigmund Freud, a psychologist interested in personality development and the treatment of personality disorders rather than in the observation of normal development. His theory describes the development of personality in terms of instinctual urges that move the individual in one direction while reality frequently attempts to impede that movement. The source of energy for these instinctual urges is sexual; accordingly, the child's development is described as a series of psychosexual stages.

The second, that of Erik Erikson, is based in large part on the theories of Freud but with several important differences. One is that Erikson deemphasized the importance of psychosexual development, focusing instead on social environment. Another is that he stressed the importance of the ego, in contrast to Freud's emphasis on the superego. A third is that Erikson concentrated on the development of a healthy personality rather than on pathological behavior.

The third theory, Jean Piaget's, focuses on cognitive or intellectual development. Piaget started his career as a biologist concerned with the problems of zoological classification and adaptation. His orientation was, therefore, biological. He later became interested in the child's mind rather than in his or her personality. His theory centers on cognitive adaptation and describes in detail the progress that a child makes as he or she acquires an increasingly logical understanding of the world. It attempts to explain this progress in terms of changes that occur in the child as a function of interactions with the environment. Piaget's theory describes children at different stages of intellectual development.

The chapter concludes with brief descriptions of behavioristic theories, ethological approaches (in particular, the work of the sociobiologists), and humanistic psychology. Behavioristic theories focus on the child's immediate behavior and on the environmental forces that affect that behavior. Sociobiology analyzes the biological basis for social behavior and attempts to explain behaviors, such as altruism, in terms of their evolutionary value. Sociobiological theories have been attacked on both logical and emotional grounds. Humanistic theory is concerned with the uniqueness of the individual child and with the development of human potential. Maslow is an important proponent of humanistic psychology.

Although children are incredibly more complicated than this chapter might suggest, they become easier to study and perhaps to understand within the more organized contexts provided by the theories presented here. These theories are not, in any real sense, complete. Nor should they be considered alternatives, for they are fully complementary.

Key Terms and Concepts

1. Theory and science
     Theory
     Prediction and control
     Scientific "attitude"
     Usefulness as a way to evalute theories

2. Theories of child development

3. Psychoanalytic approaches (Freud and Erikson)

4. Sigmund Freud
     Basic urges: survival and procreation
     Sexuality: the libido
     Personality levels
       Id: primitive, instinctual
       Ego: reality oriented
       Superego: moral/ethical conscience
     Psychosexual stages
       Oral
       Anal
       Phallic
         Oedipus complex
         Electra complex
       Sexual latency
       Genital
     Fixation and regression
     Defense mechanisms
     Criticisms of Freud's theory

33

5. Erik Erikson
        Based on Freud, but emphasizes psychosocial development
        Psychosocial stages (through adolescence)
          Trust vs. mistrust (oral)
          Autonomy vs. shame and doubt (anal)
          Initiative vs. guilt (phallic)
          Industry vs. inferiority (latency)
          Identity vs. identity diffusion (adolescence/genital)
        Life cycle

6. Cognitive approaches (Jean Piaget)
        Trained as a biologist
        Adaptation and classification
        Mechanisms of adaptation
          Assimilation
          Accommodation
        Structure and stages
          Sensorimotor (0-2 years): here and now
          Preoperational: egocentric thought
            Preconceptual (2-4 years): perception dominated reason
            Intuitive (4-7 years): illogical thought
          Concrete operations (7-11 years): conservation
          Formal operations (11-15 years): hypothetical
        Theory supported by research
        Sequence of stages more important than age

7. Behavioristic approaches
        Focus: child's needs and immediate environment
        Social learning

8. Ethological approaches
        Ethologists
        Imprinting and critical periods
        Sociobiology
          Genetic influences
          Altruism

9. Humanistic theory (Abraham Maslow)
        Uniqueness of the individual child
          Healthy personalities
          Basic needs
          Metaneeds
          Self-actualization

Short-Answer Questions

1. <u>Theory</u> <u>and</u> <u>science</u>

   a. Define <u>theory</u>.

   b. What are the ultimate goals of theorizing? Give an example.

   c. From what do theories arise?

   d. What does the <u>attitude</u> characterizing the scientific quest for explanation emphasize? Name three things.

   e. State three reasons why a variety of theories may exist to explain the same set of observations.

   f. How is the concept of <u>usefulness</u> helpful in the evaluation of a theory's adequacy?

2. <u>Theories</u> <u>of</u> <u>child</u> <u>development</u>. Five major orientations are presented in this chapter: psychoanalytic, cognitive, behavioristic, ethological, and humanistic.

3. <u>Psychoanalytic</u> <u>approaches</u> (Freud and Erikson)

4. <u>Sigmund</u> <u>Freud</u>

   a. In what field was Freud trained?

b. With what aspect of development is Freud's theory primarily concerned?

c. What two powerful tendencies motivate human behavior? Which is the most important?

d. What is the <u>libido</u>?

e. Briefly describe Freud's three levels of personality: <u>id</u>, <u>ego</u>, and <u>superego</u>.

f. Before the superego develops, how do the id and ego work together?

g. When does the superego come into its own? Through what process? Explain.

h. How does the ego mediate between the id and the superego? Give an example.

i. Identify and briefly describe the five <u>psychosexual</u> <u>stages</u> of development. Be sure to identify what part of the body produces gratification during each stage and how this is accomplished. In addition, specify what is happening with respect to the id, ego, and superego during each stage.

j. Briefly explain the <u>Oedipus</u> <u>complex</u>. Be sure to state what role the <u>castration</u> <u>complex</u> plays and how and when it is eventually resolved.

k. What is involved in the <u>Electra</u> <u>complex</u> and its eventual resolution? Be sure to state what role <u>penis</u> <u>envy</u> plays.

l. Personality development can take three alternative routes: normal, fixated, or regressed. Define and give an example of <u>fixation</u> and <u>regression</u>.

m. What are <u>defense</u> <u>mechanisms</u>? What part of Freud's system produces them and for what reason?

n. List five common defense mechanisms; define and give an example of two.

o. Identify three major criticisms of Freud's theory. Be sure to include those that led many of his followers to defect from his camp.

5. <u>Erik</u> <u>Erikson</u>

a. In what field was Erikson trained?

b. Name three important differences between Erikson's and Freud's theories.

c. Erikson identified eight stages of psychosocial development, five of which cover infancy, childhood, and adolescence. Name the first five stages, describe each, and indicate which stage in Freud's theory each parallels.

d. At the industry vs. inferiority stage, is the child latent as Freud argues? Explain.

e. How does Erikson define _identity_?

f. What is _identity_ _diffusion_?

g. Adolescence may serve as a moratorium during which children need not make irrevocable decisions concerning the self. Explain.

h. How does the term _life_ _cycle_ help explain Erikson's theory of personality development?

6. _Cognitive_ _approaches_ (Piaget)

a. In what field was Piaget trained?

b. What is the subject of Piaget's theory?

c. Identify and describe the two questions Piaget asks about human development that parallel biological questions.

d. Adaptation occurs through the interplay of two related processes-- _assimilation_ and _accommodation_. Define and give an example of each process.

e. Briefly describe the four major stages of cognitive develop-ment. Be sure to identify substages, where appropriate.

f. To what extent have research studies supported Piaget's ini-tial findings?

g. What does Piaget consider to be the most important aspect of his stage theory?

7. <u>Behavioristic approaches</u>

   a. What do behaviorists attempt to do?

   b. How is <u>social learning</u> defined?

8. <u>Ethological approaches</u>

   a. What do ethologists study?

   b. Define <u>imprinting</u> and give an example.

c. How do <u>sociobiologists</u> attempt to explain social behavior? How do they explain <u>altruistic</u> <u>behavior</u>?

d. Identify three major criticisms of ethological theory.

9. <u>Humanistic theory</u> (Maslow)

a. What is the primary concern of humanistic theory?

b. What is Maslow's major emphasis?

c. Distinguish between <u>basic</u> <u>needs</u> and <u>metaneeds</u>.

d. How are needs arranged in Maslow's system?

e. Briefly characterize the concept of self-actualization and state to what extent most college students appear to be self-actualized.

10. Review questions

   To summarize the material presented in Chapter 3, outline the
   major assumptions and variables of greatest concern for each
   of the following theories: psychoanalytic (both Freud and
   Erikson); cognitive (Piaget); behavioristic; ethological
   (sociobiology); humanistic (Maslow).

Multiple-Choice Posttest

1. The ultimate goals of a theory are to: (a) analyze and syn-
   thesize; (b) correlate and experiment; (c) observe and
   hypothesize; (d) predict and control.

2. Which of the following statements is correct? (a) Given a set of
   observations, not all theorists will arrive at the same conclusions; (b) The worst way to evaluate a theory is in terms of its
   usefulness; (c) The easiest way to evaluate a theory is in terms
   of its accuracy and truthfulness; (d) All of the above are correct.

3. Freud sees humans as having two very powerful tendencies, the urge to survive and the urge to: (a) actualize; (b) dominate; (c) love; (d) procreate.

4. The portion of the personality containing religious, ethical, and moral values in Freud's theory is: (a) ego; (b) id; (c) libido; (d) superego.

5. In Freud's system, your (   ) is to your awareness of reality as your (   ) is to your conscience: (a) ego; superego; (b) id; ego; (c) id; superego; (d) superego; id.

6. The three personality levels in Freud's system develop chronologically in which of the following orders: (a) ego, id, superego; (b) ego, superego, id; (c) id, ego, superego; (d) id, superego, ego.

7. Bob was just about to steal a record from K-Mart but stopped short when he realized that he would probably be humiliated if he got caught. In this classic Freudian conflict situation, what personality level serves as the mediator? (a) ego; (b) id; (c) libido; (d) superego.

8. The stages of psychosexual development are, in chronological order: (a) oral, anal, latency, phallic, genital; (b) oral, anal, phallic, latency, genital; (c) oral, anal, phallic, genital, latency; (d) oral, latency, phallic, anal, genital.

9. The psychosexual stage during which the child is most concerned with the genitalia is: (a) anal; (b) oral; (c) genital; (d) phallic.

10. The Oedipus complex in Freud's theory refers to: (a) a daughter's sexual love for her father; (b) a daughter's sexual love for her mother; (c) a son's sexual love for his father; (d) a son's sexual love for his mother.

11. A normal adult has a traumatic experience and subsequently becomes preoccupied with oral pleasures (smoking and eating). According to Freud, what term best explains this behavior? (a) denial; (b) fixation; (c) reaction formation; (d) regression.

12. Defense mechanisms are to the (   ) as sexual and aggressive impulses are to the (   ): (a) ego; id; (b) ego; superego; (c) superego; id; (d) superego; ego.

13. Freud's theory has been criticized on several grounds. Which of the following is not a common criticism? (a) He relied too heavily on objective measures of behavior; (b) He relied too much on sexual and agressive impulses as the basic determinants of personality; (c) His terms and concepts were ambiguous; (d) Major predictions based on his theory are frequently opposed to one another.

14. Unlike Freud, Erikson emphasized: (a) the child's sexual environment; (b) the healthy personality; (c) the role of the superego in personality development; (d) all of the above.

15. Which of the following are NOT competing tendencies in Erikson's theory? (a) autonomy vs. shame; (b) industry vs. inferiority; (c) initiative vs. guilt; (d) self-concept vs. acceptance.

16. Conflicts concerning one's behavior and bad feelings at withdrawing some of the trust they had previously placed in their environment and parents begin to emerge in young children during Erikson's stage of: (a) autonomy vs. shame and doubt; (b) industry vs. inferiority; (c) initiative vs. guilt; (d) trust vs. mistrust.

17. Erikson's stage of trust vs. mistrust closely parallels which of Freud's stages? (a) anal; (b) latency; (c) oral; (d) phallic.

18. Stephen is an adolescent who is experiencing a good deal of uncertainty in his quest to determine who he is and who he might become. This conflict is characteristic of Erikson's stage of: (a) identity versus identity diffusion; (b) industry versus inferiority; (c) initiative versus guilt; (d) trust versus mistrust.

19. Piaget was initially trained as a: (a) biologist; (b) chemist; (c) psychologist; (d) sociologist.

20. In Piaget's theory, accommodation is: (a) a reflex or other unlearned behavior; (b) the modification of an activity in the face of demands from the environment; (c) the simple exercising of an already learned behavior; (d) all of the above.

21. An infant's sucking begins to take on new forms as it comes in contact with different objects. These changes refer to Piaget's concept of: (a) accommodation; (b) assimilation; (c) conservation; (d) convergence.

22. Piaget's (   ) stage of intellectual development begins at birth and ends at age two: (a) concrete operational; (b) formal operational; (c) preoperational; (d) sensorimotor.

23. According to Piaget, during what stage does the child acquire the ability to understand numbers, classes, and relations? (a) concrete operational; (b) formal operational; (c) preoperational; (d) sensorimotor.

24. The study of human and nonhuman behavior in natural settings is the main concern of ( ) theorists: (a) behavioristic; (b) cognitive; (c) ethological; (d) humanistic.

25. Behavior that does no particular good for the individual but that protects the group to which the individual belongs is referred to as: (a) altruism; (b) genetic protection; (c) selfishness; (d) survival of the fittest.

26. Maslow's principle concern has been with the study of: (a) abnormal behavior; (b) cognitive strategies to enhance personality development; (c) the healthy personality; (d) ways to measure introversion and extroversion.

27. According to Maslow: (a) higher level needs will not be tended to until lower order needs are satisfied; (b) self-actualization is a well-defined state of happiness in which one knows that his or her potential has been achieved and maximized; (c) most people become self-actualized during adolescence; (d) all of the above.

Answers to Posttest

1. d (p. 62) 2. a (p. 63) 3. d (p. 64) 4. d (p. 66) 5. a (p. 66)
6. c (p. 65) 7. a (p. 67) 8. b (p. 68) 9. d (p. 69) 10. d (p. 69)
11. d (p. 70) 12. a (p. 71) 13. a (p. 72) 14. b (p. 73) 15. d (p. 73)
16. a (p. 73) 17. c (p. 73) 18. a (p. 75) 19. a (p. 77) 20. b (p. 78)
21. a (p. 78) 22. d (p. 79) 23. a (p. 79) 24. c (p. 82) 25. a (p. 83)
26. c (p. 84) 27. a (p. 85)

CHAPTER 4:

LEARNING AND REMEMBERING

Introduction

The study of child development involves an examination of the sequential progress children make in their efforts to deal more effectively with the world. Much of that progress occurs as a result of
acquiring information, abilities, skills, and behavioral modes through
learning. Hence, an understanding of learning is central to the study
of children.

As a division of psychology, learning is fraught with competing
and contradictory theories. It is not particularly important for the
student of child development to understand either the nature of the
specific theories or the history of the competition among them. Accordingly, Chapter 4 attempts to describe what is known--rather than
what is suspected--about learning and to present this knowledge in the
form of principles and facts rather than in the form of theories.
Thus, classical and operant conditioning are presented as models for
explaining specific kinds of learning without digression into the conflicts, past or present, among behaviorists of different varieties and
among behaviorists and cognitive and humanistic psychologists.
Numerous examples of the effects of reinforcement on children and explanations of emotional learning are presented to illustrate the basic
learning principles. The discussion then turns to social learning
theory and cognitive views of learning. In the end, it examines the
nature of human memory, particularly as it is described by a three-
stage information-processing model, which is useful in accounting for
some of the differences between child and adult memories.

Key Terms and Concepts

1. Learning: changes in behavior that result from experience

2. Types of learning
      Classical conditioning
      Operant conditioning

3. Classical conditioning (Pavlov)
      Reflexes and stimulus substitution
      Unconditioned stimulus (UCS) and unconditioned response (UCR)

46

Conditioned stimulus (CS) and conditioned response (CR)
Acquisition of emotional responses
Watson and Rayner's experiment with Little Albert

4. Operant conditioning: an introduction
Elicited (respondent) and emitted (operant) responses
The role of reinforcement
Operant vs. classical conditioning
Weisberg's study of social reinforcement and babbling
B.F. Skinner, the Skinner box, and rats
Extinction

5. Operant conditioning: reinforcement and punishment
Reinforcement is distinguished from punishment by its effects
Reinforcement: increases behavior
Reinforcer: stimulus that reinforces a response
Positive reinforcement: a reward
Negative reinforcement: removal of an unpleasant stimulus
Punishment: decreases behavior
Application of a noxious stimulus
Removal of a pleasant stimulus

6. Operant conditioning: additional details
Types of reinforcement
Primary: unlearned
Secondary: associated with primary
Generalized: reinforces almost anything, anywhere
Schedules of reinforcement
Continuous: every time the behavior occurs
Intermittent
Interval: passage of time
Ratio: number of responses
Fixed vs. random (variable)
Schedule effects
Continuous: rapid acquisition and extinction
Intermittent: maintenance of the behavior
Shaping
Selection of a target behavior
Differential reinforcement of successive approximations
Verbal conditioning

7. Biological constraints
Instinctive drift
Animals (and humans) are prepared to learn certain behaviors

8. Operant conditioning and children
General results establish the validity of operant conditioning
Lovaas's work with schizophrenic children

9. Sources of reinforcement
   Consumables, manipulatables, visual, auditory, social, token
   Premack Principle

10. Punishment
    Undesirable emotional side effects
    Conditions under which it should be used
    Practical considerations: timing, intensity, consistency, source

11. Observational learning
    Imitation and operant conditioning principles
    Vicarious reinforcement
    Manifestations
      Modeling effect
      Inhibitory effect
      Disinhibitory effect
      The Milgram study
      A variation of Milgram's study
      Eliciting effect

12. Behavior modification
    Positive reinforcement
    Extinction
    Modeling
    Fading

13. Cognitive views of learning
    Neobehaviorism: intervening or mediating variables
    Cognitivism: decision making, perception, knowing, remembering
    Information processing theories

14. Memory
    Three-stage model of information-processing
      Sensory: momentary
      Short-term: limited processing
      Long-term: a long time
    Memory processes: rehearsing, organizing, and elaborating
    Assessing memory: recalling, recognizing, and relearning

15. Development of memory
    Memory in infancy and childhood
      Few adult-child differences in sensory and short-term memory
      Long-term recall favors older children
      Strategies for organizing less adequate in young children
      Metamemory: knowledge about their memory processes develops
      as children get older
    Memory and understanding
      Generative theory: generate material
      Adding material helps us remember

1. <u>Learning</u>

    a. How is learning defined?

    b. How is learning different from growth and from the effects of fatigue and drugs?

2. What are the two basic types of learning presented in this chapter?

3. <u>Classical conditioning</u>

    a. What are the two main components of a reflex? Give an original example.

    b. Why is classical conditioning sometimes referred to as learning through <u>stimulus substitution</u>? Explain.

    c. Define <u>unconditioned stimulus</u> and <u>unconditioned response</u>. Give an original example of each.

    d. What two stimuli are repeatedly paired? Give an example.

e. How is the UCR similar to the CR?

f. What did Watson and Raynor want to show in their study with Little Albert? Identify UCS, UCR, CS, and CR.

g. Give an original example of how a child might learn to fear something in the natural environment through classical conditioning.

4. Operant conditioning: an introduction

a. What is the difference between the terms elicited and emitted? (This is important because it will help you discriminate between operants and respondents.) Give two examples of elicited behavior and two examples of emitted behavior.

b. What role does reinforcement play in operant conditioning?

c. Explain how operant conditioning differs from classical conditioning.

d. Briefly describe Weisberg's study of social reinforcement and babbling. What did the results show?

e. What name is most frequently associated with operant conditioning?

f. Define <u>extinction</u>. Give an example.

5. <u>Operant conditioning</u>: <u>reinforcement and punishment</u>

a. How is reinforcer defined?

b. How is reinforcement defined?

c. How are the procedures of <u>positive</u> and <u>negative</u> reinforcement similar? How are they different? Give an original example of each procedure.

d. What does it mean when we say that punishment is distinguished from reinforcement by its effects? Explain.

e. Describe the two types of punishment referred to by Skinner. How are they similar? How are they different? Give an original example of each.

6. Operant conditioning: additional details

a. Define and give an example of each of the following types of reinforcers: primary; secondary; generalized.

b. What is a reinforcement schedule? What is the difference between a continuous and an intermittent schedule? Between an interval and a ratio schedule? (Give an example of each.) Between a fixed and a variable (random) schedule?

You should be able to discriminate between continuous schedules of reinforcement and the various intermittent schedules. The four basic intermittent schedules are fixed ratio, fixed interval, variable ratio, and variable interval. (Note: Variable interval schedules occur very rarely in the child's natural environment, so they will not be included in the following exercises.) See if you can name the following reinforcement schedules.

c. A factory worker receives $1.00 for every 200 flanges he makes. _____

d. A slot machine pays off on the average of once every 350 times a patron deposits a dime. _____

e. A mother attends to her young infant every time the infant cries. _____

f. A secretary receives her paycheck every Friday afternoon. _____

g. Steve receives a star from his teacher for every ten math problems he solves correctly. _____

h. With respect to the effects of reinforcement schedules, how do continuous and intermittent schedules differ in terms of the ease of learning a new response? In terms of how rapidly the response undergoes extinction?

i. Briefly describe a shaping procedure. Why is shaping used? What is another name for shaping?

j. What is verbal conditioning? Briefly describe the process and state what the results of such studies demonstrate.

7. Biological constraints

a. What is instinctive drift? Give an example.

b. What does Seligman mean when he says that animals (including humans) are prepared to learn certain things (in a biological sense)? Give an example.

8. Operant conditioning and children

a. What do the general results of research with children suggest about the validity of operant conditioning procedures?

53

b. What did Lovaas et al. attempt to do with a group of schizophrenic children? How successful were they?

9. Sources of reinforcement

   a. Of the five classes of reinforcement identified by Bijou and Sturges, which is the most powerful for humans? Why?

   b. What is the Premack Principle? Give an example.

10. Punishment

   a. Name at least two undesirable side effects of punishment.

   b. Under what conditions might the use of physical punishment be justified?

   c. Name and discuss four factors one should consider in using punishment.

11. <u>Observational</u> <u>learning</u>

    a.   Briefly state how observational learning theory explains the effects of imitation in terms of operant conditioning.

    b.   What is <u>vicarious</u> reinforcement? Give an example.

    c.   How is a symbolic model different from a "normal" model? Give an example of each.

    d.   What is the <u>modeling effect</u>? How is it important in language acquisition?

    e.   What is the difference between an <u>inhibitory</u> effect and a <u>disinhibitory</u> effect? Give a real-life example of each.

    f.   What is the <u>eliciting</u> <u>effect</u>? Give an example.

12. <u>Behavior</u> <u>modification</u>. Briefly describe and give an example of:

    a.   positive reinforcement

b. extinction

c. praise-worthy model

13. Cognitive views of learning

    a. What is the basic difference between behavioristic and cognitive theories?

    b. Who has proposed perhaps the most important and comprehensive theory of cognitively oriented learning?

14. Memory

    a. Name and define the three stages of the information-processing model of memory.

    b. Distinguish among sensory memory, short-term memory, and long-term memory.

    c. Name three important memory processes.

d.   Name and define the three primary ways of assessing memory.
     State how sensitive each measure is.

15. Development of memory

     a.   How do younger and older children differ with respect to
          short-term and to sensory memory?

     b.   How do younger and older children differ in terms of long-
          term memory? What may account for this difference?

     c.   Define metamemory. How is it related to memory development?

     d.   What is the generative theory of memory? Give an example and
          explain how it is important to an understanding of memory
          development.

Multiple-Choice Posttest

1. Learning includes: (a) relatively permanent changes in behavior; (b) the effects of drugs on behavior; (c) the effects of fatigue on behavior; (d) all of the above.

2. A bouquet of roses is sprinkled with strong Indian pepper. The demure young lady to whom the bouquet is presented sneezes violently. On subsequent occasions, she is presented with other bouquets that have also been sprinkled with pepper. Eventually, the mere sight of roses is sufficient to make her sneeze. In this example, the lady's sneezing in response to the pepper is: (a) a conditioned response; (b) a conditioned stimulus; (c) an unconditioned response; (d) an unconditioned stimulus.

3. ( ) behavior is learned through the consequences it produces; ( ) behavior is reflexive: (a) Respondent; respondent; (b) Respondent; operant; (c) Operant; operant; (d) Operant; respondent.

4. Which of the following terms is not associated with operant conditioning: (a) elicit; (b) extinction; (c) reinforcement; (d) shaping.

5. If you give a child a penny for each correct answer during a math test and the child starts producing more correct answers, you would be: (a) negatively reinforcing errors; (b) positively reinforcing correct answers; (c) both (a) and (b) ; (d) neither (a) nor (b) .

6. Social prestige, money, and praise are common examples of ( ) reinforcers: (a) consumable; (b) generalized; (c) primary; (d) vicarious.

7. If a child receives one token for every five problems solved correctly, the child is being reinforced on a ( ) schedule of reinforcement. (a) continuous; (b) fixed interval; (c) fixed ratio; (d) variable ratio.

8. Which of the following schedules of reinforcement is likely to lead to the fastest rate of extinction: (a) continuous; (b) fixed ratio; (c) variable interval; (d) variable ratio.

9. The process of differentially reinforcing successive approximations to a desired target behavior is called: (a) disinhibition; (b) modeling; (c) shaping; (d) the Premack Principle.

10. You notice that a 7-year-old prefers recess to any of the academic subjects, and therefore you decide to allow the 7-year-old to go to recess only after completing two pages of math. What behavioral concept are you capitalizing on in this example? (a) extinction; (b) modeling; (c) shaping; (d) the Premack Principle.

11. Which of the following statements is correct? (a) Although it is possible to classically condition emotional responses in infants, attempts at operant conditioning with infants have typically failed; (b) Autistic and schizophrenic children are typically unresponsive to operant conditioning procedures; (c) The principle of instinctive drift refers to the observation that many animals who are trained to perform arbitrary responses eventually revert to behaviors more characteristic of their species; (d) All of the above are correct.

12. Which of the following statements is correct? (a) Intense physical punishment is typically less effective than mild physical punishment; (b) The Premack Principle states that behaviors that are engaged in frequently need no reinforcement; (c) The use of physical punishment is often accompanied by undesirable emotional side effects; (d) All of the above are correct.

13. As Charlie approaches graduation from kindergarten, he begins to wear a tie like the first graders. If you ask him, he'll tell you he's doing it 'cause he saw that kids who wear ties got to buy their lunches at school (something he's always wanted to do but has never done). In this example, the opportunity to buy lunch at school is a/an (   ) reinforcer: (a) eliciting; (b) manipulatable; (c) negative; (d) vicarious.

14. Rod loves to drive his van at 80 miles an hour even though the speed limit is 55. Whenever he observes someone else being stopped, however, he slows down. This is an example of the (   ) effect: (a) disinhibitory; (b) eliciting; (c) inhibitory; (d) modeling.

15. Ivan frequently throws spit balls in school and sometimes even shoots paper clips with rubber bands. His younger brother, Tora, has observed Ivan several times and now begins to throw pencils in his classroom. This is an example of the (   ) effect: (a) disinhibitory; (b) eliciting; (c) inhibitory; (d) modeling.

16. A major difference between behavioristic theory and cognitive theory is that the latter deals with (   ) whereas the former does not: (a) classical conditioning; (b) independent variables; (c) operant conditioning; (d) thinking and knowing.

17. Which of the following is not one of the stages of the three-stage information-processing model of memory: (a) long-term; (b) recognition; (c) sensory; (d) short-term.

18. Memory that involves more elaborate cognitive processing and that may be retained indefinitely refers to (   ) memory; (a) conceptual; (b) long-term; (c) sensory; (d) short-term.

19. If a psychologist were to ask you to tell her everything you could remember about your date last night, she would be using which of the following ways to measure memory? (a) generation; (b) recall; (c) cognition; (d) relearning.

20. Which of the following statements is correct? (a) In general, research has found that young children are better at short-term and sensory memory tasks than older children and adults; (b) Older children typically use more sophisticated processing skills in memory tasks than younger children; (c) Research shows that one of the most effective ways to hinder correct recall is to generate material not present in the original memory task; (d) All of the above are correct.

21. Knowledge about one's memory and one's memory processes is referred to as: (a) cognitivism; (b) conceptual imagery; (c) generative capacity; (d) metamemory.

Answers to Posttest

1. a (p. 92) 2. c (p. 94) 3. d (p. 96) 4. a (p. 98) 5. b (p.100)
6. b (p.101) 7. c (p.102) 8. a (p.101) 9. c (p.104) 10. d (p.109)
11. c (p.105) 12. c (p.109) 13. d (p.112) 14. c (p.114) 15. b (p.115)
16. c (p.116) 17. b (p.118) 18. b (p.118) 19. b (p.119) 20. b (p.121)
21. d (p.121)

CHAPTER 5:

PRENATAL DEVELOPMENT AND BIRTH

Introduction

The most orderly and predictable phase of human development occurs prior to birth. As they age, individuals become increasingly different, not only physiologically but also psychologically.

Chapter 5 traces the course of prenatal development, beginning with fertilization of the ovum, progressing through the embryo stage (two to eight weeks following conception), and terminating with the fetus stage. The symptoms by which a woman can determine that she is, in fact, pregnant are detailed along with the physical characteristics of the child in utero during the ten lunar months preceding birth. Research indicates that the fetus is sensitive to sound, that it may be conditioned prior to birth, that it may be affected by maternal emotions, and that it is highly susceptible to influence from a wide variety of drugs, including narcotics. In addition, there is some evidence to indicate a correlation between social class and the incidence of premature births. It appears that maternal health is intimately linked with the well-being of the fetus and with the probability that it will come to term. Although prenatal development is highly regular and predictable, a large number of factors can be beneficial or harmful to intrauterine development.

With respect to the process of birth itself, there apparently is some complex instinct in subhuman mammals that compels expectant mothers to seek out safe places in which to give birth to their young. That same instinct appears to provide them with a rather complicated body of knowledge regarding what they should do during birth and how they can best look after their offspring to increase their chances of survival. Thus, a mother dog will remove the pup's umbilical cord, clean its nose and mouth, stimulate its breathing while cleaning it roughly with her tongue, and eventually move the pup toward one of her life-supporting nipples. Humans no longer appear to need--or to possess--these instincts. Approximately 266 days after conception, a child is born.

The latter part of the chapter describes the three stages of labor, beginning with dilation of the cervix and culminating with the expulsion of the afterbirth. Various childbirth techniques are outlined and birth is described from two perspectives: the mother's and the child's. The chapter concludes with a brief discussion of prematurity.

61

Key Terms and Concepts

1. Conception: the zygote is formed

2. Pregnancy
     Early signs
     Sure signs

3. Prenatal development
     Gestation period
     Life in utero
     Fertilized ovum: the zygote (conception through one week)
     Embryo (one to eight weeks)
       Implantation in the uterine wall
       Rapid development of key organs and structures
       Placenta forms
       Umbilical cord attaches
     Fetus (third month to birth)
       Length increases at a constant rate
       Weight increases more toward the end of gestation

4. Factors affecting prenatal development
     Life in utero
       Fetal conditioning
       Relation between mother's and child's nervous systems
     Maternal emotions
       Chemical theory
       Possible genetic influences
       Nervous rat mothers (Thompson)
     Drugs
       Animal study results difficult to generalize to humans
       Critical time: embryonic stage
       Teratogens: drugs that cause fetal defects
       Nicotine
       Alcohol: in moderation, perhaps
       Narcotics: harmful
     Maternal health
       Rubella
       Age of the mother
     Maternal malnutrition
       Greatest single cause of fetal death
       Effects on intellectual development
       May be most critical during late fetal development
     Social class
       Premature birth: leading cause of infant death
       High correlation between social class and premature birth
     Rh incompatability

5. Childbirth
    Obstetrics: Hippocrates' contribution
    Clinical view of labor
        First stage: cervix dilates, contractions begin, amniotic
            sac breaks
        Second stage: the child is born
        Third stage: afterbirth is expelled
        Types: abortion; immature; premature; mature; postmature
        Size and gestation descriptors: small for date (SFD);
            average for date (AFD); large for date (LFD)
        Caesarian section
    Neonatal scales: Apgar
    Labor from the mother's viewpoint
        Natural childbirth
        Lamaze method
        Leboyer method
    Effects of sedatives
    Labor from the child's viewpoint
        Use of forceps
        Prolapsed cord
        Anoxia
        Birth trauma
    Prematurity
        Correlated with malnutrition, social class, and poverty
        Measured intelligence appears lower
        Human contact appears important

Short-Answer Questions

1. Conception

    a. What is a zygote?

    b. What is the process by which the zygote is formed?

2. Pregnancy

    a. Name four early signs of pregnancy, and state when each is
       typically present.

b. Name three ways pregnancy can be verified.

3. Prenatal development

   a. What is a gestation period? How long does it typically last in humans? Explain in terms of both lunar and calendar months.

   b. Suppose you are a mature ovum (egg). Trace your steps from the time you mature until you are successfully impregnated and implanted in the uterine wall. Tell precisely where you met your partner and where you went after you met him.

   c. When does a zygote officially become an embryo? Explain.

   d. What is the umbilical cord? To what is each end of the umbilical cord attached?

   e. What is the placenta? Identify at least two functions that it performs.

f. The mother's circulatory system is not directly connected to
    the child's circulatory system. Explain then how the prenate
    gets food and oxygen.

g. Briefly describe the prenate at the end of the embryonic
    stage (two lunar months or six weeks). How is the prenate
    similar to an adult?

h. What is the earliest month of development in which the
    prenate would likely survive if born prematurely?

i. Fetal growth primarily involves changes in length and weight.
    The length of the fetus increases at a relatively constant
    rate throughout pregnancy. Explain how this is different
    from the rate at which the fetus gains weight.

j. Why is brain development particularly important during the
    last three months of pregnancy?

4. Factors affecting prenatal development

    a. Give two reasons why factors affecting prenatal development
        are frequently confused and difficult to study.

b. Briefly describe the procedure Spelt used to <u>condition</u> the fetus <u>in</u> <u>utero</u>. Why did he test his bell before he paired it?

c. Why has some doubt been cast on Spelt's findings?

d. Describe the physical relationship of the mother's nervous system to that of the unborn child.

e. Briefly state how a mother's anxiety during pregnancy appears to affect the fetus.

f. Briefly describe Thompson's experiment on the effects of maternal emotions on newborn rats. Be sure to identify the independent and dependent variables. What did the results of the study show?

g. What did Hockman discover about the effects of stress and anxiety on offspring? On mothers?

h. Explain why it is usually difficult to generalize findings about drug studies from animals to humans.

66

i. During what stage of prenatal development is the unborn child most susceptible to serious structural damage? Explain. Why are external influences less important during later development?

j. Name three common effects of nicotine on prenatal development.

k. What is the _fetal alcohol syndrome_? What condition produces it?

l. How do narcotics affect the fetus?

m. What is _rubella_? What is its common name? Name two defects rubella may cause in the fetus or newborn.

n. What are the optimal years for a woman to have a child? Name two potential hazards for the fetus in a pregnancy after the optimal years.

o. Maternal nutrition is a worldwide problem of great magnitude.
    Experimental evidence suggests that the diet of a pregnant
    woman affects the intelligence of the fetus.   Briefly
    describe an experiment using human subjects that supports
    this statement.

p. Why may the effects of malnutrition be considered par-
    ticularly critical during late fetal development and early
    childhood?

q. What is the greatest cause of fetal death?

r. What is the greatest single cause of infant death?   What is
    the relation between this cause and social class?

s. What is Rh incompatability? How is it typically treated?

5. Childbirth

a. What is an obstetrician and when might you visit one?   What
    did Hippocrates contribute to the field of obstetrics, and
    when did he make this contribution?

b. List the labels for a fetus according to the length of time spent in utero, from shortest to longest.

c. Define the following classifications in terms of weight and gestation: small for date; average for date; large for date.

d. Briefly describe the three stages of labor and state how long each one lasts.

e. What is the amniotic sac? Explain its function during prenatal development.

f. What is a Caesarian section? State two reasons why one might be performed.

g. What is the Apgar Index? What does a score of four or less indicate?

h. What is <u>natural</u> childbirth? Briefly describe the Lamaze method and the Leboyer technique.

i. Name at least two differences between children delivered to mothers who were given anesthetics and children delivered without anesthetics.

j. Explain how each of the following might influence the infant at birth: the use of forceps; prolapsed cord; anoxia.

k. Does the child respond emotionally to birth? Explain why or why not. How is this related to the theory of a psychological birth trauma?

l. How is <u>prematurity</u> usually defined? What are some possible causes? What does the available evidence indicate about the effect of social status on prematurity?

m. What is one of the most obvious effects of prematurity? What are some other effects? Do all premature babies suffer disadvantages? Explain.

n. What does the Scarr-Salapatek and Williams study suggest might be done with premature babies?

Multiple-Choice Posttest

1. The technical term for a newly fertilized ovum is a/an: (a) embryo; (b) fetus; (c) neonate; (d) zygote.

2. Which of the following is among the first signs of pregnancy in the human female? (a) a distended abdomen; (b) cessation of menses; (c) detection of the fetal heart beat; (d) dilation of the vagina.

3. The prenate officially becomes an embryo: (a) at the end of the second lunar month when arm and limb buds are present; (b) when the egg is fertilized; (c) when the egg leaves the ovary; (d) when the zygote is implanted in the wall of the uterus.

4. Which of the following is not characteristic of the prenate at the end of the embryonic stage? (a) curled shape characteristic of the fetus; (b) differentiated internal organs; (c) the embryo is clearly recognizable as a human; (d) 10-12 inches in length and 2-3 pounds.

5. The fetus is attached to the mother by a long thick structure containing two arteries and a vein called the: (a) amniotic sac; (b) lanugo; (c) placenta; (d) umbilical cord.

6. Which of the following statements is correct? (a) A child born any time before the sixth month of pregnancy has a relatively poor chance for survival; (b) The prenate gains most of its weight during the last three months of pregnancy; (c) The prenate's length increases at a relatively constant rate throughout pregnancy; (d) All of the above are correct.

7. Which of the following statements concerning the effects of maternal emotions on offspring is correct? (a) Anxiety in pregnant rats has more serious consequences for the mothers than for the offspring; (b) Human mothers who are anxious during pregnancy frequently have children who are calmer and less irritable than nonanxious mothers; (c) Offspring of anxious mother rats do not outgrow their anxiety (d) All of the above are correct.

8. Drugs and other substances that cause fetal defects are called: (a) delirium tremens; (b) hormones; (c) Rh antibodies; (d) teratogens.

9. Which of the following statements is incorrect? (a) Alcohol consumption by a pregnant mother may produce "fetal alcohol syndrome."; (b) Nicotine increases fetal heart rate and is correlated with premature birth; (c) Rat studies are very useful in determining the effects of drugs on humans, because both organisms are mammals; (d) The prenate is most susceptible to damage by drugs during the embryonic stage of development.

10. The most frequent cause of fetal death is: (a) maternal malnutrition; (b) rubella; (c) drugs consumed by the mother; (d) maternal anxiety.

11. Which of the following is most clearly correlated with premature birth: (a) alcohol consumption; (b) Down's syndrome; (c) low social class; (d) maternal anxiety.

12. Which of the following Rh combinations causes the greatest risk of fetal death if not corrected? (a) Mother: rh-positive; fetus: rh-positive; (b) mother: rh-positive; fetus: rh-negative; (c) mother: rh-negative; fetus: rh-positive; (d) mother: rh-negative; fetus: rh-negative.

13. During prenatal development the amniotic sac: (a) acts as a shock absorber and bathes the child; (b) provides nourishment for the child; (c) serves as a source of nerve connections from the mother; (d) all of the above.

14. The average duration for labor in humans is: (a) 1-2 hours; (b) 5-6 hours; (c) 12-14 hours; (d) 1-2 days.

15. The third stage of labor involves: (a) dilation of the cervix; (b) expulsion of the afterbirth; (c) passage of the child into the birth canal; (d) passage of the child out of the birth canal.

16. Most physicians would consider a score of 2 on the Apgar index: (a) as nothing special, since 2 is the average; (b) cause for serious alarm; (c) ridiculous, since the Apgar index goes from 0 to 1; (d) the sign of an extremely healthy newborn.

17. The prepared childbirth technique that teaches expectant mothers a variety of breathing and relaxation exercises is called the ( ) method: (a) Brutus; (b) Caesarian; (c) Lamaze; (d) Leboyer.

18. A shortage of oxygen to the brain is called: (a) anoxia; (b) a prolapsed cord; (c) Rh incompatibility; (d) teratogenesis.

19. Which of the following statements in incorrect? (a) Abnormalities occur more frequently among premature babies than among mature babies; (b) One factor implicated in prematurity is maternal malnutrition; (c) The best way to treat premature babies is to keep them in isolation until they reach normal, mature birth weight; (d) The most common cause of death among premature babies is respiratory failure.

Answers to Posttest

1. d (p.128) 2. b (p.128) 3. d (p.130) 4. d (p.131) 5. d (p.131)
6. d (p.131) 7. a (p.137) 8. d (p.138) 9. c (p.137) 10. a (p.139)
11. c (p.141) 12. c (p.142) 13. a (p.144) 14. c (p.144) 15. b (p.145)
16. b (p.147) 17. c (p.148) 18. a (p.151) 19. c (p.153)

CHAPTER 6:

ATTACHMENT AND SOCIAL-EMOTIONAL DEVELOPMENT

Introduction

Chapter 6 begins with a discussion of the bidirectionality of influence between parent and child and a consideration of individual
differences as these influences are reflected in characteristic infant
states and infant emotions (crying, fearing, and smiling). It
describes attachment in monkeys and in humans, stranger anxiety, and
the effects of maternal separation and institutionalization on the
child before turning to a consideration of the father. He too is a
figure of attachment for his children, although attachment to the
father appears to be qualitatively different than attachment to the
mother. Changing family roles and the increasing participation of
fathers in child rearing may alter this situation in the future.

Key Terms and Concepts

1. Bidirectionality of influence
   Parents influence children and vice versa
   Difficulties in studying parent-child relationships

2. Infant states
   Individual differences are pronounced
   Environmental and genetic influences
   Bidirectionality of influence

3. Infant emotions
   Interpret with caution
   Present at birth
   Watson's three emotions: fear, rage, and love
   Crying
   Fearing
   Smiling: three stages
     Laughter
     Blind infants and their mothers: reactions to filmed vs.
       actual mothers
   Bidirectionality of influence works for both closeness
       and distance

4. Attachment
       Difficult to investigate
         Definition and measurement problems
         Controlled experiments (unethical with humans)
       Mother-infant bonding
         Appears to be augmented by increased contact immediately
              following birth
       Bowlby's ethological analysis of attachment
       Learning theory analysis of attachment: mutual reinforcement
       Fathers: occurs at a young age when the opportunity to do so
              is present

5. Attachment among monkeys: studies of maternal deprivation
       Surrogate mothers
       Independent and dependent variables
       Results: monkeys prefer cloth

6. Strangers and separation
       Stranger anxiety
       Security blankets
       Institutionalized children
         Marasmus
         Mothering or lack of perceptual stimulation
       Maternal separation
         Severity of effect increases with the age of the infant
         Critical period hypothesis

7. The whole infant

Short-Answer Questions

1. Bidirectionality of influence

    a. To what does the term bidirectionality of influence refer?
        Give an example.

    b. State at least two reasons why parent-child relations are
        difficult to study. Remember: Not only are there marked in-
        dividual differences among parents but also among infants.

2. Infant states

    a. What are infant states? Give an example. How do they relate to individual differences among infants?

    b. Are infant states affected by the environment? Give an example to support your answer.

    c. Why is it difficult to relate infant states to subsequent individual differences? Give an example that illustrates the bidirectionality of influence.

3. Infant emotions

    a. Give two reasons why statements about infant emotions must be interpreted with caution.

    b. Name three distinct emotional responses identified by Watson in newborns.

    c. Briefly describe what is known about infant crying.

    d. Briefly describe what is known about how infants react when they are afraid.

e. Briefly describe the three stages of smiling in infants
    When does laughter begin to develop? What types of stimula
    tion produce it?

f. How do blind infants differ from normal infants in terms of
    smiling? How do mothers of blind infants differ from mothers
    of sighted infants in terms of how they treat their infants?

g. What do the results of studies comparing infant responses to
    filmed mothers versus actual mothers suggest about the impor-
    tance of visual contact?

h. Bidirectional influence is present in many different situa-
    tions. Give an example illustrating how it may lead to
    distance between parent and child.

4. Attachment

a. Cite two major reasons why attachment is difficult to study
    in humans.

b. To what does the term <u>mother-infant</u> <u>bonding</u> refer? What leads to its development?

c. What effect does increased physical contact between a mother and her newborn appear to have on later interactions? At age one month? At age one year?

d. Briefly describe Bowlby's ethological view of attachment.

e. What two aspects of the mother's behavior appear to be most highly related to her child's attachment to her? Is quality or quantity of stimulation more important?

f. How does learning theory attempt to explain attachment?

g. Briefly describe at least three important changes that have recently altered our conception of the father's role in in-fant attachment.

h. Briefly summarize the current status of the father's role in infant attachment.

5. <u>Attachment</u> <u>among</u> <u>monkeys</u>: <u>the Harlows' study</u>

a. What are surrogate mothers? Give an example.

b. What were the independent variables in the Harlows' study?

c. Name and define two ways the Harlows measured the dependent variable. Be specific.

d. What did the results of the Harlows' study show with respect to each dependent variable? Be specific.

e. What cautions should be taken in interpreting the Harlows' results?

6. <u>Strangers</u> <u>and</u> <u>separation</u>

a. Briefly summarize what is known about <u>stranger</u> <u>anxiety</u>.

b. What is a <u>security blanket</u>? Briefly describe its role in the development of many infants.

c. What does evidence from studies of institutionalized children suggest about the effects of maternal deprivation?

d. Define <u>marasmus</u>.

e. Why must the results of maternal separation studies be interpreted with caution?

f. What facets of infant development does maternal separation apparently affect? How are its effects related to the age at which separation occurs? How is this related to the notion of a critical period in humans?

Multiple-Choice Posttest

1. Which of the following statements is correct?
(a) Bidirectionality of influence refers to the wide variety of biological factors that influence epigenetic unfolding; (b) Infant states are unaffected by environmental conditions during the first three months of life, suggesting that they are largely genetically based; (c) Parent-child relations are frequently difficult to study because of the marked individual dif-

ferences that exist among both parents and children; (d) All of the above are correct.

2. Research on infant states indicates that: (a) later individual differences among children are a direct result of inherited initial differences; (b) the environment can bring about changes from one state to another; (c) they are remarkably consistent from one infant to another; (d) all of the above.

3. Which of the following statements is correct? (a) Although there are many individual differences, most mothers appear remarkably sensitive to infant cries; (b) Fear of strangers ordinarily manifests itself during the first six months of life; (c) Whenever infants cry, it nearly always follows the same pattern: a long wail, followed by a period of breath-holding; (d) All of the above are correct.

4. Which of the following statements is correct? (a) Although blind infants do not appear to smile as much as normal infants, their mothers feel more attachment for their babies than do mothers of otherwise normal babies; (b) Research with filmed and actual mothers has shown that physical presence is more important than visual contact for most three- and four-year-old children; (c) The bidirectionality of influence appears to operate on parent-child relations to produce both distance and closeness; (d) All of the above are correct.

5. Which of the following statements is correct? (a) It is difficult to study the effects of separation and social isolation in humans because controlled experiments in this area are unethical; (b) Mother-infant bonding appears to be augmented by close physical contact shortly after birth, but the effects of this closeness disappear by the end of the first year; (c) Mother-infant bonding refers to the attachment of the embryo's umbilical cord to the mother's placenta during prenatal development; (d) All of the above are correct.

6. Which of the following statements is correct? (a) Bowlby's ethological analysis of attachment holds that bonds between the mother and child are the end-product of an evolutionary process; (b) Learning theory maintains that attachment results from the mutual reinforcement the mother and infant provide each other; (c) Quantity of stimulation is more important than quality of stimulation in determining an infant's attachment to her mother; (d) All of the above are correct.

7. Which of the following statements is correct? (a) Mother-infant bonding appears to be augmented by close physical contact shortly after birth, but the effects of this closeness disappear by the end of the first year; (b) Research shows that in general fathers tend to provide more social stimulation while mothers provide more caretaking functions; (c) Young infants (age seven to thirteen months) typically become more attached to their mothers than to their fathers, but the trend reverses as the child grows older, particularly among males; (d) All of the above are correct.

8. In the Harlow experiment of maternal deprivation, the independent variable was: (a) the amount of time the infant spent embracing the models; (b) the response of the infant to a fear-producing stimulus; (c) whether the surrogate was covered with wire or cloth; (d) all of the above were independent variables.

9. Fear of strangers: (a) is common among many infants; (b) occurs at about two months of age; (c) occurs most among children who have had contact with the greatest number of people; (d) all of the above.

10. Depression, sadness, weeping, and increased susceptibility to disease due to maternal deprivation is called: (a) anoxia; (b) marasmus; (c) reverse bonding; (d) separation anxiety.

11. Which of the following statements is correct? (a) Most older infants display anxiety when either their mother or father leave them in a novel situation; (b) Maternal separation has an adverse affect on most aspects of the infants development; (c) Maternal separation is more serious for older infants (4-8 months) than for younger infants (1-3 months); (d) All of the above are correct.

Answers to Posttest

1. c (p.158) 2. b (p.160) 3. a (p.161) 4. c (p.164) 5. a (p.165)
6. d (p.165) 7. b (p.170) 8. c (p.166) 9. a (p.172) 10. b (p.174)
11. d (p.174)

CHAPTER 7:

COGNITIVE AND PERCEPTUAL DEVELOPMENT IN INFANCY

Introduction

Newborns are not pretty cherubs. While they are physically help-
less, they are far from being insensitive to environmental stimulation. Chapter 7 describes their reactions to light, sound, smell,
taste, and touch.   In addition, it details their motor development
during infancy (until age two). The chapter concludes with an examination of the child's cognitive development during Piaget's stage
of sensorimotor development.

Key Terms and Concepts

1. Neonates
    Height (20 inches) and weight (7 1/2 pounds) at birth
    Most rapid gains during first six months

2. The orienting response
    Cardiac acceleration and deceleration; galvanic skin response
    Index of attention
    Used to measure discrimination ability

3. Behavior in the newborn: most is reflexive
    Survival value: sucking and head turning (rooting)
    Vegetative: sneezing, swallowing, vomiting
    Other: Babinski, Moro, palmar (grasping), swimming, stepping

4. Motor development
    Cephalocaudal (head to foot)
    Proximodistal (inward-outward)
    Sits, creeps, stands, walks
    Cultural factors

5. Perceptual development
    Visual
       Pupillary reflexes
       Fixation time: the Fantz study
       Depth perception: develops as early as 1 1/2 months
    Sounds: discriminates sounds

Odors: reacts to powerful, unpleasant odors
Taste: least well developed
Pain: remarkably insensitive

6. Cognitive development (Piaget)
    Schemes: infant's simple behaviors
    Assimilation and accommodation
    Object concept
    Acredolo's study of infants and the here and now environment:
       from egocentricity to objectivity

7. Piaget's substages of sensorimotor development
    Substage 1 (0-1 month): Exercising reflexes - looking,
       grasping, sucking, crying
    Substage 2 (1-4 months): Primary circular reactions
    Substage 3 (4-8 months): Secondary circular reactions
    Substage 4 (8-12 months): Purposeful coordinations -
       object concept
    Substage 5 (12-18 months): Tertiary circular reactions
    Substage 6 (18-24 months): Mental representation - cognitive

    Deferred imitation
    Enactive representation

Short-Answer Questions

1. Neonates

    a. What is a neonate? Briefly describe one.

    b. What are the physical (length and weight) dimensions of the
        typical neonate?

    c. During what six-month period does the infant gain the most
        weight? Specifically state how much.

2. The orienting response

   a. What is an orientation reaction? Give an example.   How can
      it be measured?

   b. Give two examples of how orientation reactions are commonly
      measured in infants.

   c. Of what value are orientation reactions to child psy-
      chologists?

   d. Briefly describe how orientation reactions have been used to
      measure the neonate's ability to discriminate different
      sounds.

3. Behavior in the newborn: most is reflexive

   a. The neonate's behavior can be classified into one of two
      general response classes: reflexive and unintentional. Give
      an example of each.

b. Describe each of the following reflexes. Identify the
    stimulus that elicits each reflex and indicate (1) whether it
    is vegetative and (2) whether or not it has any survival
    value for the infant: sucking; rooting (head-turning); Moro;
    sneezing; Babinski; Darwinian (palmar grasp).

4. Motor development

    a. What are norms? Give an example.

    b. What does it mean when we say that the sequence of motor
        abilities in children appears relatively invariant? Give an
        example.

    c. Identify the age (in months) at which each of the following
        (norms) occurs in the typical infant: stand alone; sit with
        support; walk alone; sit alone; creep; climb stairs.

    d. How is the principle of proximodistal development different
        from cephalocaudal development? Define and give an example
        of each.

e. Briefly summarize at least one study that has investigated cultural differences in motor development.

5. Perceptual development

a. Perception in the neonate exists in more varied forms than previously thought. Describe two sources of evidence suggesting that the newborn's visual system is fairly well developed shortly after birth.

b. What did Frantz measure in his study of visual perception in newborns? That is, what was the dependent variable? What visual stimulus produced the largest effects? What do the results of this study demonstrate?

c. Briefly state what is known about depth perception in very young infants.

d. Briefly describe the neonate's sensitivity to each of the following: sound; odor; taste; pain.

6. Cognitive development (Piaget)

a. Define scheme.

b. Explain how infants <u>assimilate</u> and <u>accommodate</u> aspects of their environment. Give examples illustrating how these two processes operate.

c. What is the <u>object concept</u>? Give an example. When does it develop?

d. Briefly describe Acredolo's study of infants and their here and now environment. Explain how the results of the study relate to the concepts of egocentricity and objectivity.

7. <u>Sensorimotor development</u>

a. How long does the sensorimotor stage last? What do <u>sensori</u> and <u>motor</u> mean?

b. Identify two major characteristics of each of the six substages of sensorimotor development.

Substage 1 -

Substage 2 -

Substage 3 -

Substage 4 -

Substage 5 -

Substage 6 -

c. Define and give an example of each of the following:

    primary circular reactions -

    secondary circular reactions -

    tertiary circular reactions -

d. What is the <u>matchbox</u> <u>problem</u>? What can it indicate about the development of an eighteen- to twenty-four-month-old child?

e. Define and give an original example of <u>deferred</u> <u>imitation</u>.

f. What is <u>enactive</u> <u>representation</u>? Give an example.

Multiple-Choice Posttest

1. At birth, the typical male neonate weighs ( ) pounds and measures ( ) inches long: (a) 5-1/2 - 15; (b) 7-1/2 - 20; (c) 9-1/2 - 20; (d) 9-1/2 - 15.

2. Which of the following statements is correct? (a) The average neonate doubles in weight during the first six months of life; (b) The infant gains weight at a constant rate from birth to two years of age; (c) The typical neonate is virtually insensitive to external stimulation prior to one week of age; (d) All of the above are correct.

3. Which of the following would not be considered an orientation reaction? (a) an increase in heart rate: (b) changes in pupil size; (c) galvanic skin response (GSR); (d) sneezing.

4. Tickling a neonate's soles will give rise to the ( ) reflex: (a) Babinski; (b) head turning (rooting); (c) Moro; (d) sucking.

5. Which of the followig neonatal reflexes has the least survival value for the infant? (a) head turning; (b) Moro; (c) sucking; (d) vomiting.

6. The typical infant is first able to walk unaided at ( ) months: (a) 5; (b) 10; (c) 15; (d) 20.

7. Most children are able to control movement of their arms before they can effectively coordinate their legs and feet. This is an example of the principle of ( ) development: (a) cephalocaudal; (b) Darwinian; (c) medial-lateral; (d) proximodistal.

8. When shown various circular patterns, newborns 10 hours to five days old prefer the: (a) closest; (b) most brightly colored; (c) most complex; (d) simplest.

9. Perception of depth is present at least from the time the infant can: (a) crawl; (b) see; (c) sit with support; (d) walk.

10. The human newborn: (a) can discriminate between different sounds; (b) is more sensitive to odor than to taste; (c) visually follows slow-moving objects; (d) all of the above.

11. During Piaget's sensorimotor period, children: (a) do not have an internal, symbolic representation of their world; (b) interact with their world largely through motor activity; (c) understand their world primarily through their sensation of it; (d) all of the above.

12. A child's ability to imagine things even when they are not perceived directly is referred to by Piaget as: (a) concrete representation; (b) deferred imitation; (c) object concept; (d) symbolism.

13. A child accidentally begins to suck on her big toe; the sensation of the suction serves as a stimulus for its repetition, and the child continues to suck her toe. This is an example of: (a) a primary circular reaction; (b) a secondary circular reaction; (c) enactive representation; (d) object concept.

14. Primary circular reactions come about as the result of: (a) accidental responses; (b) deliberate responses; (c) imitative responses; (d) reflexes.

15. Internalizing an object as part of one's cognitive structure is referred to as: (a) a tertiary circular reaction; (b) deferred imitation; (c) enactive representation; (d) symbolism.

Answers to Posttest

1. b (p.183)   2. a (p.183)   3. d (p.184)   4. a (p.185)   5. b (p.185)
6. c (p.187)   7. a (p.186)   8. c (p.189)   9. a (p.190)   10. d (p.191)
11. d (p.194)   12. c (p.193)   13. a (p.196)   14. a (p.196)   15. c (p.199)

Crossword Puzzle

Across

3. The placenta and other membranes expelled during the third stage of labor (_____ birth)
5. Tickling the middle of the infant's sole elicits this reflex
8. Part of the uterus that dilates during the first stage of labor
10. Childbirth without anesthetics
11. Development from head to foot
13. Name for an umbilical cord caught in the birth canal
16. To miscarry before the twentieth week of pregnancy
17. Wicked-looking, clamplike instrument sometimes used to deliver a baby

18. Process of separating fetus and other membranes from mother's body

Down

1. Restricted supply of oxygen to the brain
2. Most infants are able to do this without aid at seven months
4. Physiological shock that some say accompanies birth
5. Birth in which buttocks appear first
6. Placing an object in an infant's hand elicits this reflex
7. Most births after 37-42 weeks of gestation are classified this way
9. Technical term for a newborn
12. A type of movie, particularly prevalent around Halloween
14. What you might expect a two-year-old to call his father
15. A neonate's startled reflex to a sudden loud noise

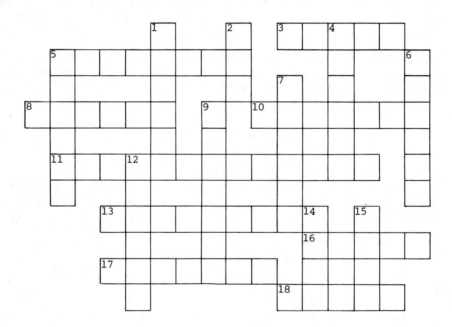

Solution to Crossword Puzzle

Across		Down	
3.	after	1.	anoxia
5.	Babinski	2.	sit
8.	cervix	4.	trauma
10.	natural	5.	breech
11.	cephalocaudal	6.	palmar
13.	prolapsed	7.	mature
16.	abort	9.	neonate
17.	forceps	12.	horror
18.	labor	14.	dada
		15.	Moro

CHAPTER 8:

LANGUAGE DEVELOPMENT

Introduction

The attribute that appears to most clearly differentiate humans from other animals is their ability to speak. Although animals can communicate, as far as we know none has yet developed a language. One of the most significant and important aspects of infant development is the acquisition of language. It is truly amazing that this incredibly complex body of information and skills can be mastered as rapidly as it is. Beginning at birth with only the ability to utter meaningless and uncontrolled sounds, many children progress to a point where, by the age of two, they can converse with other humans employing a vocabulary of 250 or more words in various two-word combinations. Chapter 8 describes what is known about the acquisition of language, pointing out some interesting and significant gaps in our knowledge. It concludes with an examination of the role of language in thought.

Key Terms and Concepts

1. Language and communication

2. A definition of language
    Displacement
    Meaning
    Productiveness

3. Elements of language
    Phonemes
    Morphemes
    Syntax
    Prosody

4. Language and nonhumans
    Washoe: American sign language
    The Premacks' plastic shapes

5. Language development in humans
    Communication without language: common gestures
    Active vs. passive vocabulary
    Normative vocabulary tests

94

6. Prespeech: development of meaningful speech sounds
   Crying, gestures, and babbling
   Babbling: all sounds are produced
   Repetitious babbling
   The first word: difficult to determine what and when
   Two-word sentences: at eighteen months of age

7. Speech: from first word to adultlike sentences
   Sentencelike words (holophrases)
   Modification (two-word sentences)
   Structure
     Multiple-word sentences
     Complete subjects and predicates
   Operational changes: conjunction, embedding, and
     permutation
   Categorization (parts of speech used correctly)
   Complex structure
     Further refinements and elaboration
     Phase structure: arrange words in meaningful expressions
     Transformational rules: active-passive

8. Learning Theory
   Reinforcement and imitation
   Imitation cannot adequately explain errors in grammar

9. Chomsky's language acquisition device (LAD)

10. Caretaker-infant interactions
    Bidirectionality of parent-child influence
    Fine tuning

11. A biological theory
    Motor and language development are closely allied
    Sequence of both is highly predictable

12. Additional details
    Sex differences
    Twins
    Stuttering
    Brain-to-body weight ratio

13. Language and thought
    The Whorfian hypothesis
    The Plyes study: verbal facilitation of learning
    Bernstein's language codes: social influences
      Restricted
      Elaborated
    White and black children in school: different language codes

Short-Answer Questions

1. Language and communication

    a. What is the relationship between language and communication? Which is necessary for the other?

    b. What does language add to communication? Give an example.

    c. Why is a parrot's mimicking not considered communication?

2. A definition of language

    a. In your own words, give a definition of language.

    b. Brown describes three essential characteristics of language: displacement, meaning, and productiveness. Define each.

3. Elements of language. Define and give an example of:

    a. phoneme -

    b. morpheme -

c. syntax -

d. prosody -

4. Language and nonhumans

   a. Although early attempts failed to teach monkeys and chimpan-
      zees language, the Gardners devised an ingenious way to ap-
      proach the problem. What did they use to teach language to
      their chimpanzee, Washoe?

   b. Briefly describe how the Premacks taught language to chimpan-
      zees.

5. Language development in humans

   a. Could we communicate without language? Name two universal
      gestures and state what they typically signify. Of what sig-
      nificance is the fact that these gestures appear to occur in
      all cultures?

   b. What is the difference between an active and a passive
      vocabulary? Which develops first? Which is typically
      larger?

c. On what basis are most <u>normative</u> vocabulary tests con-
    structed? Explain why the test data must be interpreted with
    caution.

6. <u>Prespeech stage</u>

    a. What is the <u>prespeech</u> stage and what time period does it
        span?

    b. What is <u>babbling</u>? How many different sounds do infants
        typically produce as they babble?

    c. How is repetitious babbling important to language acquisi-
        tion? Explain.

    d. At approximately what age do children typically utter their
        first meaningful word? Why is it difficult to determine
        precisely when this occurs?

    e. What parts of speech are the child's first words likely to
        be? Give two or three examples.

7. Speech stage

   a. The term speech stages is best described as a progression
      from sounds to words to grammar. Beginning with the child's
      first meaningful word (holophrase), there are six sequential
      stages. What is a holophrase? Give an example illustrating
      how a holophrase functions.

   b. Modification is the second stage of speech development. What
      are two-word sentences? Give an example. Why are they fre-
      quently hard to interpret?

   c. What is the significance of the transition from modification
      to structure? What types of sentences are involved at the
      structure stage?

   d. What is the most significant aspect of the operational
      changes stage? Give an example.

   e. What is the main characteristic of the categorization stage?

   f. Briefly describe what happens during the complex structure
      stage.

8. <u>Learning</u> <u>theory</u>

Briefly describe how learning theory attempts to explain language
development. Identify at least one way in which it is an incomplete theory of language development.

9. <u>Chomsky's</u> <u>LAD</u>

What is a <u>language</u> <u>acquisition</u> <u>device</u> (LAD)? What role does it
play in Chomsky's view of language development?

10. <u>Caretaker-infant</u> <u>interactions</u>. Briefly describe how interactions
between a mother and her infant influence language development.
Emphasize the bidirectionality of the parent-child influence.

11. <u>A</u> <u>biological</u> <u>theory</u>

a. How closely allied are simple motor and language development?
What does this suggest about the genetic basis of both?

b. From text Table 8.3, briefly describe what the child is
capable of doing in terms of both motor and language development at each of the following ages:

six months -

one year -

two years -

four years -

12. Additional details

a. Briefly state what is known about each of the following with
respect to language development:

sex difference -

twins -

stuttering -

b. Is there any correlation between brain weight and intelligence? Explain. What is the significance of the brain-to-body
weight ratio?

13. Language and thought

a. What is the Whorfian hypothesis?

b. Briefly describe Pyles's study of the effects of names on learning. How did the three study groups differ? What did the results show? How were the results similar to those reported by Lefrancois about his grandmother?

c. Bernstein has used the terms <u>restricted</u> and <u>elaborated</u> language codes. Define and give an example of each code. How is the difference between restricted and elaborated language reflected in social class differences? What kind of child typically suffers when exposed to the school environment? Why? Explain?

d. How did Baratz (1969) determine that black children are not less advanced in their language development than white children?

Multiple-Choice Posttest

1. Which of the following statements is correct? (a) Animals are incapable of communication; (b) Communication involves the construction of words from arbitrary sounds; (c) Language facilitates sophisticated forms of communication; (d) Language is essential for communication.

2. One key characteristic of language is productiveness. This refers to: (a) how verbal expressions relate to the object for which they stand, to the mental images evoked, or to the emotional reaction produced; (b) our ability to create new combinations of words and phrases; (c) our ability to represent objects and events that are not currently present; (d) the rules that govern the grammar of a language.

102

3. The grammar of a language is referred to as its: (a) morphemology; (b) phonemology; (c) prosody; (d) syntax.

4. The Gardners were successful in teaching language to their chimpanzee by using: (a) a computer terminal so the chimpanzee could type words rather than having to say them orally; (b) poker chips of different colors to denote different words; (c) sign language; (d) simple, one-syllable words.

5. Passive vocabulary develops ( ) active vocabulary and is ( ) in size than active vocabulary: (a) after; larger; (b) after; smaller; (c) before; larger; (d) before; smaller.

6. Babbling is: (a) a necessary step in language acquisition; (b) the means by which infants acquire control over the sounds they produce; (c) the repetitious practicing of single sounds; (d) all of the above.

7. It is commonly accepted that children can understand and utter their first word at the age of ( ) month(s) : (a) one; (b) six; (c) twelve; (d) eighteen.

8. Two-word sentences are characteristic of the ( ) stage of speech development: (a) categorization; (b) modification; (c) operational changes; (d) structure.

9. Implicit understanding of the grammatical function of various words and phrases (for example, correct usage of parts of speech) develops during the ( ) stage of speech development: (a) categorization; (b) modification; (c) operational changes; (d) structure.

10. A ( ) rule is one that allows us to change a passive sentence into an active one. (a) phase structure; (b) syntactical; (c) transformational; (d) Whorfian.

11. Chomsky's model of early language development: (a) argues that imitation and reinforcement play an important role in language development; (b) believes children are born with a neurological capacity that corresponds to grammar (called a language acquisition device); (c) contends that children learn syntax by practicing language acquisition devices; (d) all of the above.

12. Which is the correct chronological order for the following events: (1) sitting without aid, (2) vocalizing, primarily of crying, (3) uttering two-word sentences, and (4) walking with the aid of an adult. (a) 1, 2, 3, 4; (b) 1, 2, 4, 3; (c) 2, 1, 3, 4; (d) 2, 1, 4, 3.

13. Which of the following statements is correct? (a) Compared to their peers, twins are typically advanced in their language development; (b) Research results about sex differences in language acquisition are often contradictory, suggesting that there may be no reliable sex differences; (c) Stuttering is typically considered abnormal, particularly among young (3- to 4-year-old) children; (d) All of the above are correct.

14. Which of the following statements is correct? (a) In general, the higher the brain-to-body weight ratio, the lower the intelligence of the organism; (b) It is possible to estimate the intelligence of an organism from its brain weight alone; (c) There is no correlation between brain weight and intelligence; (d) All of the above are correct.

15. The Whorfian hypothesis holds that: (a) thoughts determine language; (b) language determines thoughts; (c) language and thoughts are not closely related; (d) restricted language codes are more difficult to interpret than elaborated language codes.

16. Evidence from a number of experiments suggest that: (a) familiar objects are easier to recall than unfamiliar objects; (b) unfamiliar objects that are given names are easier to remember than unfamiliar objects that are left nameless; (c) both (a) and (b) ; (d) neither (a) nor (b) .

17. According to Bernstein, middle- and upper-class children use ( ) language codes: (a) elaborated; (b) repetitious; (c) restricted; (d) Whorfian.

Answers to Posttest

1. c (p.206) 2. b (p.207) 3. d (p.208) 4. c (p.210) 5. c (p.213)
6. d (p.214) 7. c (p.215) 8. b (p.217) 9. a (p.217) 10. c (p.219)
11. b (p.220) 12. d (p.223) 13. b (p.226) 14. c (p.228) 15. b (p.227)
16. c (p.227) 17. a (p.229)

CHAPTER 9:

COGNITIVE DEVELOPMENT IN EARLY CHILDHOOD

Introduction

Chapter 9 takes a brief look at physical and motor development in early childhood and then turns to a discussion of intellectual development as described by Piaget. Lefrancois looks in turn at preconceptual and intuitive thinking--the two sequential substages of preoperational thought--noting that the preschool child's thinking is somewhat egocentric, perception dominated, and intuitive rather than logical. He points out the tremendous advances that children make between two and six years of age, but makes it clear that the six-year-old child's thinking is still replete with errors in logic.

In the end, the chapter discusses attempts to intervene in the cognitive, social, and emotional development of the preschooler. Eight different preschool projects, selected from among countless others, are discussed not only in terms of methods used but also in terms of the results they produce. Although the long-term results of preschool intervention programs have been disappointing, at least insofar as we have been able to measure them, they may have been useful in suggesting what should be done and how. In addition, it is quite possible that we simply have not detected or measured some highly positive social and emotional benefits of intervention programs. In any case, it appears likely that the greater emphasis in education for the immediate future will be at the preschool rather than at the school level, although both are currently gaining in importance.

Key Terms and Concepts

1. Physical growth between two and six years of age
       Growth rates slow down
       Baby fat decreases
       Head-to-body ratio decreases

2. Motor development
       Sequential acquisition of locomotor and grasping skills
       Copying geometric shapes
       Dressing skills
       Physical and motor development are correlated

3. Cognitive development: Piaget's preoperational stage
   Preconceptual thinking
   Intuitive thinking

4. Preconceptual thinking (ages two to four)
   Sensation and activity vs. symbols
   Preconcepts: incomplete concepts
   Transductive reasoning: single attributes
   Syncretic reasoning: changing criteria

5. Intuitive thinking (ages 4 to 7): immediate comprehension
   Limited ability to classify: class inclusion problems
   Egocentric thought: values of the child
   Perception dominated: the appearance of things

6. Research and implications
   Piaget's sequence validated across cultures
   Ages of attainment vary with individual children
   Preoperational children achieve a great deal

7. Preschool education: an overview
   Many programs may not produce long-term effects
   Effects often difficult to measure

8. Nursery schools: most prevalent form of preschool education

9. Early Training Project (Gray and Klaus)
   Works with children from impoverished backgrounds
   Provides great amounts of stimulation
   Initial gains impressive but diminish over time

10. Parent Education Project (Gordon)
    Works with children and parents in the home
    Based on Piaget

11. The Ypsilanti project
    Derived directly from Piaget's work
    Sensorimotor to operational thought
    Program starts at an early age
    Mothers are involved

12. Project Head Start: extensive federal program started in 1964
    Designed for children from deprived backgrounds
    Summer preparation for entering school
    Many different approaches
    Initially, not an overwhelming success
    Project continues: more consistency and some benefits

13. Earlier intervention (Caldwell)
    Involves children prior to age three
    Moderate success but not for those under age three

14. The Bereiter-Engelmann approach
    Content oriented: reading, language drills, math
    Achievement gains reported

15. The Montessori Method
    Ideas, materials, ideology
    Learning stems from perception
    Individual liberty and independence
    Critics
       Too much emphasis on materials
       Ignores social development

16. Current status of preschool education
    Well-defined criteria for evaluation are needed
    Bronfenbrenner's sequential intervention strategy
       Considers the family as a child-rearing unit
       Preparation for parenthood
       Before children come
       First three years of life
       Preschool years (4-6)
       Elementary school years (6-12)
    Continued emphasis at the entry level in the future

Short-Answer Questions

1. Physical development

    a. Explain how children's rate of weight gain between birth and two years compares with their rate of weight gain between two and six.

    b. How does the child's distribution of fatty tissue change between infancy and age six? Why does this change occur?

c. How does the ratio of head-to-body size change between birth and age six? Be specific.

2. Motor development

   a. The infant's most significant motor achievement is learning how to walk. At what age does this typically occur (on the average)? Name two other things infants are learning at about the same time.

   b. Indicate the earliest age (according to Gesell) at which the normal child can do each of the following: lace shoes; copy a circle; copy a triangle; button clothes; copy a cross.

   c. Give an example illustrating the relationship between physical and motor development.

3. Cognitive development (Piaget). Why is the preschooler's intellectual development characterized as preoperational? What are the two substages of preoperational thought? What ages does each span?

4. Preconceptual thinking

   a. What is the major difference between the sensorimotor child and the preconceptual child? Give examples illustrating this difference.

b. What is a preconcept? Give an example of a child's use of
    preconceptual thought.

c. Two major features of preconceptual thought are transductive
    and syncretic reasoning. Define and give original examples
    of each.

5. Intuitive thinking

    a. How does intuitive thinking differ from logical thinking?
        Give an example and state when the intuitive substage begins
        and ends.

    b. The intuitive child has a limited ability to classify.   Give
        an original example that illustrates this statement.

    c. What is egocentricity as applied to intellectual development?
        Give an original example.

d. What does it mean when an intuitive child is characterized as being <u>perception</u> <u>dominated</u>? Give an example.

6. <u>Research</u> <u>and</u> <u>implications</u>

a. What types of evidence are used to support the validity of the sequence of Piaget's stages?

b. Why is it difficult to determine when children typically attain certain cognitive skills? Does Piaget consider age of attainment important? Why or why not?

c. Why are <u>preoperational</u> children most frequently described in terms of what they cannot do rather than on the basis of their achievements? Why does Gelman consider this to be a misleading description of preschoolers?

7. <u>Preschool</u> <u>education</u>: <u>an</u> <u>overview</u>

a. What is the most striking feature of the preschooler's environment?

b. Preschool programs frequently do not produce enduring effects when compared with programs involving children who have not had preschool experience. Outline two possible reasons why preschool gains may not be enduring.

8. Nursery schools. Nursery schools are the most prevalent form of preschool education in the United States. Briefly describe them and the type of activities they typically emphasize. What aspects of development do they affect most beneficially?

9. Early Training Project (Gray and Klaus)

    a. How did the four groups in the Gray and Klaus study differ? That is, what was the independent variable?

    b. What was the project's basic assumption (hypothesis)?

    c. What were the results in terms of IQ gains at the end of the study? At the end of four years?

10. Parent Education Project (Gordon). Briefly describe the Parent Education Project. How does it differ from typical preschool programs?

11. The Ypsilanti project

    a. On whose theory is the Ypsilanti project based?

    b. Briefly describe the project's "total cognitive framework." How is it important?

    c. Explain how a simple activity such as "juice time" could be used to foster intellectual development.

    d. The benefits of the project have been attributed to two basic assumptions underlying its program. Outline those assumptions.

12. Project Head Start

    a. Project Head Start, begun in 1964, probably has been the most extensive preschool program ever undertaken in the United States. How and why was it formed?

    b. Why are the overall results of Project Head Start difficult to evaluate?

c. Identify at least three reasons why the program has not been overwhelmingly successful.

d. What is the current status of the Head Start program?

13. <u>Earlier</u> <u>intervention</u> (Caldwell)

a. What is Caldwell's "Inevitable Hypothesis?"

b. Briefly describe Caldwell's program and its results.

14. The <u>Bereiter-Englemann</u> <u>approach</u>

a. Briefly explain what the Bereiter-Englemann approach involves.

b. What are the three curriculum areas in the program? Why are they stressed?

c. How was the program's success measured? What did the results of the project indicate?

15. The Montessori method

    a. Briefly describe the following components of the Montessori system: the idea; the material; the ideology.

    b. Name two criticisms of the Montessori method and discuss their validity.

16. Current status of preschool education

    a. What is needed to make a thorough analysis and review of preschool education programs?

    b. What is the single fundamental assumption of Bronfenbrenner's sequential intervention strategy?

    c. Briefly describe Bronfenbrenner's five stages.

    d. Why does Lefrancois believe that the major emphasis in education in the immediate future will be made at the entry level?

Multiple-Choice Posttest

1. With respect to physical development between the ages of two and six, which of the following statements is correct? (a) Approximately 1/4 of the six-year-olds body is head; (b) Children gain weight at a faster rate between two and six than between birth and two; (c) Six-year-olds typically have a proportionately smaller amount of fatty tissue than two-year-olds; (d) All of the above are correct.

2. Piaget's (   ) stage of intellectual development begins at about age two and ends at about age seven: (a) concrete operational; (b) formal operational; (c) preoperational; (d) sensorimotor.

3. The sensorimotor period stresses (   ) while the preoperational stage involves (   ): (a) activity; images; (b) preconcepts; concepts; (c) preconceptual thought; intuitive thought; (d) syncretic reasoning; transductive reasoning.

4. A child who believes that objects that resemble each other are, in fact, the same object is demonstrating what Piaget calls (   ) thought: (a) concrete operational; (b) formal operational; (c) preoperational; (d) transductive.

5. Syncretic and transductive logic are examples of what Piaget calls (   ) thought: (a) enactive; (b) intuitive; (c) preconceptual; (d) sensorimotor.

6. Boys have hair; girls have hair; therefore, girls are boys. This is an example of what Piaget refers to as: (a) enactive representation; (b) intuitive representation; (c) transductive reasoning; (d) syncretic reasoning.

7. A five-year-old boy tells you that his preschool class has more boys than children. This illustrates that: (a) he is limited in his ability to classify correctly; (b) he is egocentric; (c) his thought process is perception dominated; (d) all of the above.

8. According to Piaget, egocentricity is one characteristic of (   ) thought: (a) conservative; (b) enactive; (c) intuitive; (d) preconceptual.

9. Which of the following statements is correct? (a) Most cross-cultural studies have found that the age of attainment of the various cognitive stages described by Piaget is valid; (b) Piaget is more concerned with when children acquire various cognitive skills than he is with the order in which they are attained; (c) The preoperational stage is most often described in terms of what children cannot do, rather than in terms of their achievements; (d) All of the above are correct.

10. The Early Training Project (Gray and Klaus): (a) compared the effects of their program on children from impoverished background with its effects on middle-class children; (b) reported initial gains for the experimental groups that continued to increase for several years after the end of the study; (c) was based on the assumption that the deleterious effects of an impoverished background are directly tied to the amount and variety of stimulation a child receives; (d) All of the above are correct.

11. The Ypsilanti project: (a) argues that the deleterious effects of impoverished backgrounds are linked directly to problems of malnutrition; (b) attempts to provide a remedial program in the child's home, thus involving parents; (c) believes that preschool programs are most likely to succeed if they involve both the infant and the mother; (d) all of the above.

12. Which of the following preschool education programs is based heavily on Piaget's work? (a) Caldwell's Earlier Intervention Program; (b) Project Head Start; (c) The Early Training Project (Gray and Klaus); (d) The Ypsilanti Project.

13. Project Head Start: (a) has been criticized because it treated children outside the context of the home and failed to follow up when children entered regular school; (b) reported initial gains in IQ test scores that continued to increase for several years following the end of the study; (c) is based heavily on Piaget's theory of cognitive development; (d) all of the above.

14. The Bereiter and Engelmann approach to preschool education: (a) holds that all learning stems from perception; (b) is designed to teach culturally disadvantaged children specific skills; (c) reported initial gains in IQ and IQ achievement test scores that continued to increase for several years following the end of the study; (d) all of the above.

15. The Montessori method: (a) holds that all learning stems from perception; (b) has been criticized for relying too heavily on interaction with materials rather than with peers; (c) stresses individual liberty and is concerned with the development of human potential; (d) all of the above.

116

16. Bronfenbrenner's sequential intervention strategy: (a) advocates cognitively-oriented preschool programs that also involve parents; (b) believes that all learning stems from perception; (c) emphasizes the child's psychosocial and personality development through the use of sense training; (d) all of the above.

Answers to Posttest

1. c (p.237) 2. c (p.240) 3. a (p.241) 4. c (p.241) 5. c (p.241)
6. c (p.242) 7. a (p.243) 8. c (p.242) 9. c (p.246) 10. c (p.248)
11. c (p.251) 12. d (p.250) 13. a (p.251) 14. b (p.254) 15. d (p.255)
16. a (p.258)

CHAPTER 10:

THE FAMILY'S INFLUENCE

Introduction

Chapter 10 examines the influence of the family on the social, emotional, and intellectual development of the child. In general, the important child-rearing variables appear to relate to the quality of parent-child interactions rather than to specific practices. The importance of love cannot be overstated. About birth order, there is less certainty because of some conflicting research, although first-born and only children appear to have an advantage in intellectual development and performance. The Zajonc-Markus model, about which there is some debate, explains these differences in terms of the higher intellectual climate of homes with more adults and older children than homes with only one adult and/or a number of very young children. Homes with only one adult--the great majority of which are headed by a female--have often been associated with adjustment problems of various kinds. It is fairly clear that separation, divorce, and death have profoundly saddening and sometimes highly disturbing effects on children. The long-term effects of being reared in a one-parent family are not always clear and are far from predictable for individual cases; nor are intact families always conducive to optimal social, emotional, and intellectual development.

The chapter concludes with a consideration of child abuse. Reported instances of child abuse may represent the tip of a frightful iceberg. Several factors appear to be implicated--the age, sex, and disposition of the child; the family's socioeconomic level; parental stress; and whether a parent was abused as a child. Nevertheless, none of these factors justifies such abuse.

Key Terms and Concepts

1. The family: the most powerful socializing agent in the first six years of a child's life

2. Origins of the family
   Nuclear families
   Extended families

3. The contemporary family
   Nuclear families predominate
   One-parent families
      Affects one out of seven children under six years of age
      Result primarily from divorce

4. Family influences
   External
   Bidirectional
   Difficult to study because of private nature of the family

5. Parent-child relations
   Difficult to study; child care and the child's personality are
      hard to measure
   Demanding, but warm and loving relations are correlated with
      high self-esteem and creativity

6. Child-care advice: (assumes child malleable and vulnerable)
   Freudian model: emotional experiences important
   Behavioristic model: reinforcement and punishment
   Prediction harder than after-the-fact explanations
   Studies have produced ambiguous results
   The age of permissiveness based on false assumptions
   Love appears to be critical

7. Birth order
   Galton: first to notice advantages of first-borns
   Need to achieve is higher in first-borns
   Possible effects of social interactions

8. Family size
   An only child is similar to a first-born
   Siblings
   Zajonc-Marcus model: achievement test scores
      Average intellectual climate of the home
      May not be predictive, particularly for individuals

9. One-parent families
   Affect or will affect close to half of all American children
   Father absence: three factors are hard to separate
      Father's actual role
      Change in mother's role
      Change in economic condition of the family
      Freud says it is critical during ages four to six
   Research: most is retrospective
      Some evidence that one parent has an effect
      Cannot generalize to individuals or make causal statements
   Hetherington's study of girls from one-parent families
      Intact, divorced, and widowed families

Age of child when father lost important
Wallerstein and Kelley's study of middle-class divorced children
Studied preschoolers; young and old school children
Some adverse effects for all groups
Caution: studies like this apply only on the average

10. Child abuse
Historical: Infanticide and abandonment
U.S. estimate of 250,000 cases a year is probably too low
Cuts, bruises, and fractures most common forms
Affects older children more
Males more likely to be physically punished
Socioeconomic factors
Child factors also implicated
Many who abuse were themselves abused
Parental stress and the use of punishment

Short-Answer Questions

1. The family. Why is the family considered to be the most powerful socializing agent in a young child's development?

2. Origins of the family

   a. Distinguish and give examples of nuclear and extended families.

   b. Which is more prevalent in contemporary U.S. society?

3. The contemporary family

   a. What is average size of the typical nuclear family?

b. About how many children under the age of six are currently being raised in one-parent families?

c. What factor has contributed most to the decline in the number of nuclear families?

4. Family influences

a. Why is the family unit considered a dynamic source of in-fluence?

b. Give an example of bidirectional influence within the family unit.

c. Identify three reasons why the family's influence is dif-ficult to measure.

5. Parent-child relations

a. Identify two factors that make parent-child relations par-ticularly difficult to study.

b. What two factors appear to be positively correlated with a child's self-esteem and creativity?

6. Child-care advice

    a. Briefly characterize the two models that have dominated our
        thinking about child-care advice. What do both models as-
        sume?

    b. What problems have been encountered in studies attempting to
        identify specific factors in parent-child relations? Give an
        example.

    c. What single variable appears most highly related to adjust-
        ment and maturity?

    d. Many researchers now agree that no specific practices should
        be advocated, but that some general parental characteristics
        may have positive or negative effects. Briefly state what
        Baumrind says about these effects, paying particular atten-
        tion to her analysis of "permissive" child-rearing practices.

7. Birth order

    a. What did Galton observe about birth order?

    b. Briefly compare first- and later-born children in the fol-
        lowing areas: need to achieve; language development.

c. How can social interaction be used to explain the effects of
    birth order?

8. Family size

    a. How are only children similar to first-born children in terms
        of development?

    b. Name three reasons why the effects of family size are hard to
        study systematically.

    c. Briefly describe what is known about the effects of siblings
        on development.

    d. What observation led Zajonc and Markus to propose their
        family-size model of intellectual development? How does the
        model determine the intellectual climate of the home?

    e. What validity does the Zajonc-Markus model have?   Name at
        least two limitations of the model.

9. One-parent families

    One-parent families currently affect or will affect close to half
    of all American children. Most result from divorce and are
    headed by women. Most of the studies of one-parent families in-
    dicate that divorce and separation may have harmful effects for
    the child(ren), but it should be remembered that these are state-
    ments of the average effect. Many one-parent families effec-
    tively overcome the loss of one parent. Furthermore, there is no
    way to determine the adequacy of parenting in intact homes.

    a. Name three factors that should be considered in an anlysis of
        father absence.

    b. According to Freud, when may fathers be particularly crucial?
        Why?

    c. How have researchers typically tried to analyze the effects
        of father absence? What two cautions should be taken in in-
        terpreting the results of such studies?

    d. Briefly describe Hetherington's study of girls from intact,
        divorced, and widowed homes. What did the results of the
        study show, particularly with respect to the girls' age when
        they lost one parent?

e. Briefly describe the studies of Wallerstein and Kelley on the effects of divorce on children of different ages. What did the results indicate for each of the age groups studied and in general?

10. <u>Child abuse</u>

a. About how many cases of child abuse are reported annually in the United States? Why should this be considered a low estimate of the actual number of instances?

b. What are the most prevalent forms of abuse?

c. Briefly state how each of the following factors may contribute to child abuse:

age of the child -

sex of the child -

socioeconomic level of family -

disposition and/or behavior of the child -

parent who was also abused as a child -

excessive use of punishment as a child-rearing practice -

parental stress -

Multiple-Choice Posttest

1. A family group consisting of mother, father, children, aunts, uncles, grandparents, and various assorted relatives is defined as a/an (   ) family: (a) advantaged; (b) communal; (c) extended; (d) nuclear.

2. The decline in proportion of nuclear families is due primarily to an increase in: (a) divorce rates; (b) family size; (c) the number of unmarried women who keep their babies; (d) the number of widowed parents.

3. Which of the following statements is correct? (a) One reason the family is hard to study as a social unit is because it is a highly private entity; (b) The family unit is typically a dynamic (as contrasted with static) source of social influence; (c) The nature of social influence in most families is bidirectional; (d) All of the above are correct.

4. Parent-child relations are hard to study because: (a) it is difficult to determine whether the child or the parent determines a particular child-rearing practice (for example, permissiveness,); (b) parent's and children's behavior are often inconsistent in different situations; (c) the child's personality is frequently hard to measure; (d) all of the above.

5. Which of the following statements is correct? (a) Both the Freudian and behavioral models of child-care advice stress the vulnerability and malleability of the child; (b) Most research on specific child-care techniques have found consistently reliable results, particularly in the areas of feeding schedules in infancy and toilet training; (c) Parental characteristics that appear to be highly correlated with successful adjustment in their children are permissiveness and self-control; (d) All of the above are correct.

6. Which of the following parental variables appears to be most highly related to adjustment? (a) consistency; (b) discipline; (c) love; (d) maturity.

7. Which of the following statements is correct? (a) Differences between first-born and later-born children are typically explained in terms of parent-child interactions; (b) First-born children tend to be less curious than later-born children; (c) Twins develop language more rapidly than non-twins; (d) All of the above are correct.

8. Which of the following statements is correct? (a) An only child shows many of the advantages and disadvantages of a first-born child; (b) On the average, second-born children receive more attention than first-born children because they compete harder for it; (c) Second-born and later-born children are typically more achievement oriented than first-born children because they are constantly being compared with their older sibling(s) ; (d) All of the above are correct.

9. Zajonc and Markus observed that measured IQ scores among high school seniors has been dropping during the 1960s and early 1970s. They attributed this to: (a) changes in the socioeconomic and political climate of the U.S. during that time; (b) the changing intellectual climate of the home due to families with little space between children; (c) the use of permissive child-rearing practices during this time span; (d) all of the above.

10. Most studies of the effects of one-parent families: (a) are applicable primarily to individual children and should not be generalized to groups of children; (b) are retrospective; that is, they occur after the fact; (c) have provided psychologists with a wide range of highly useful techniques to predict when a child from a one-parent home will experience adjustment difficulties; (d) all of the above.

11. In their study of children from recently divorced families, Wallerstein and Kelly found that: (a) girls at all age levels adjusted more readily to the divorce than boys; (b) regardless of age level, the effects were manifested in many children in their later adjustment; (c) young children (2-6) were significantly affected whereas older children (7-10) were only marginally affected; (d) all of the above.

12. Which of the following statements is correct? (a) Child abuse is more prevalent among very young children than among older children; (b) Cuts, fractures, and bruises are common manifestations of child abuse; (c) Parents who abuse their children are more likely to use extreme physical violence with an older male child than with a young male child; (d) All of the above are correct.

Answers to Posttest

1. c (p.264) 2. a (p.266) 3. d (p.266) 4. d (p.266) 5. a (p.268)
6. c (p.269) 7. a (p.271) 8. a (p.271) 9. b (p.274) 10. b (p.276)
11. b (p.278) 12. b (p.279)

CHAPTER 11:

SOCIALIZATION, PLAY, AND SEX ROLES

Introduction

Adequate adjustment to an environment requires that individuals become socialized and learn to behave in acceptable and expected ways. Children become socialized through the influence of their parents, peers, school, religion, and the media. They learn to behave according to their sex. They learn that some behaviors are bad and that some are good. They imitate a wide variety of models. They become more or less susceptible to group pressure. They may or may not be profoundly influenced by television. Research on the effects of television, although unclear, is by no means completely favorable or completely unfavorable.

Chapter 11 discusses the process of socialization. It looks first at social pressure, social imitation, minority groups, and the effects of television as an environmental and socializing force. Next, it considers the manifestations of play in childhood and the importance of imagination and fantasy. Adults do not play very often or very well; some do not play at all. They live and they work. Children do not work very well or very often; most do not work at all. They live and they play. Everything they do is done solely for the pleasure inherent in the activity. Psychologists can gain considerable insight into the lives of young children by examining their play behavior. This part of the chapter describes the types of play engaged in by young children, including practice games, rule-regulated games, and symbolic games in various combinations. The type of game a child plays is related to his or her physical, social, personality, and intellectual development.

In conclusion, the chapter departs from fantasy and looks at the hard realities of sex roles and sex stereotypes. Times are changing.

Key Terms and Concepts

1. The child's social environment
     Culture, family, peer groups
     Television, books, school

2. Socialization
     Culture: mores, traditions, beliefs, values, ways of behaving,

and rules
Genetic influences: invariant across races and cultures
Environmental factors: <u>extent</u> to which they influence behavior
Transmission of culture from generation to generation

3. Minority groups
Defined in many ways: ethnic, economic, social, religious
Disadvantages
Deprivation index

4. Group pressure
Related to the size and personality of the group
Less pressure in our society
No single code
Consequences are remote
Asch's experiment
Role of the confederate
Many subjects conform to pressure

5. Social imitation
Modeling by parents and others
Symbolic models often important to children

6. Television
A national pastime, especially among children
Violence
Measures in a laboratory setting hard to generalize to real life
A prevalent theme in children's programs
Some benefits in the area of language and general information
Prosocial behavior can also be promoted (e.g., "Mister Rogers",
"Sesame Street")
Viewing patterns: the young (children and adults) and the elderly
Short-term increases in aggressive behavior can be promoted by
having children view violent programs
Long-term effects unclear
Four models of the effects of TV violence
Cathartic: releases hostility
Catalytic: initiates or facilitates hostility
Imitation: serves as a model for hostility
Apathy: no effect
More carefully controlled studies are needed

7. Play
Play vs. work
<u>Sensorimotor play</u>: for the sheer sensations involved
<u>Imaginative play</u>: a constructive process
People, activities, objects
Daydreaming: common among preschoolers
Imaginary playmates

Implications of imagination
May have beneficial effects
Possibly related to fairy tales
Social play: interaction
Parallel vs. cooperative play
Sex differences are evident in children's play

8. Sex roles: behaviors, attitudes, and personality characteristics
Sex typing: learning sex-appropriate behavior
Mead's study of three New Guinea tribes
Masculinity and femininity culturally determined
Possible genetic effects due to homogeneous cultures

9. Sex typing and sex roles
Traditional stereotypes
Female liberation movement: an impact
Determinants: biological, family, culture
Criteria for genetic influence
Aggression
Possibility of bidirectional influence
Sex differences (on the average; not applicable to individuals)
Identification of masculine and feminine characteristics
Girls appear to have superior verbal skills
Achievement orientation and affiliation
Parental attitudes of central importance
Cross-cultural studies: no sex differences
Times are changing

Short-Answer Questions

1. Social environment. Name six important factors in the child's
social environment.

2. Socialization

    a. Define socialization.

    b. Give a brief definition of culture. Use your own words.

c. Those aspects of the human condition most closely determined by genetic factors are least variable across cultures. Explain this statement and give an example.

d. What is the significant question concerning the influence of culture on development?

3. Minority groups

a. What are minority groups? Name at least three ways they can be identified.

b. Briefly describe the plight of many minority groups.

c. Briefly describe the results of social deprivation studies and their relation to self-concept.

4. Group pressure

a. What is the relationship between the size of a group and pressure to conform? Give an example illustrating this relationship.

b. State two reasons why our society does not exert as much pressure to conform as do less technological societies.

c. Briefly describe Asch's experiment. Be sure to identify the
    independent and dependent variables and to indicate what the
    results of his study demonstrated.

5. Social imitation. Several psychologists (e.g., Bandura) strongly
    emphasize the process of social learning to explain, in part, how
    culture is transmitted.

    a. What is imitation? What role does the imitation model play?

    b. What is a symbolic model? Give an original example.

6. Television

    a. How extensive is television viewing in the United States,
        particularly among young children?

    b. Briefly state what evidence exists to support the contention
        that television induces violence in children. Why is it
        probably unrealistic to generalize from the Bandura studies
        to real-life situations? Give two reasons.

    c. How do TV viewers typically differ from nonviewers?

d. What evidence is there to suggest that a child, particularly a socially disadvantaged child, may benefit from television viewing?

e. To what extent are children's TV programs dominated by violence? How does this compare with adult programming?

f. What three age groups watch the greatest amount of TV?

g. What evidence is there that violence on TV induces short-term aggression in children?

h. Why has it been difficult to determine the long-term effects of TV? What kind of study would be required to answer this question?

i. Why must statements of the causal effects of TV be interpreted cautiously?

j. What evidence is there to suggest that TV promotes prosocial behavior?

k. Briefly describe each of the following models of the impact
    of televised violence on children:

    cathartic -

    catalytic -

    imitation -

    no effect -

l. What is the most valid conclusion we can presently make con-
    cerning the effects of TV on children?

7. <u>Play</u>

    a. What is the primary difference between <u>work</u> and <u>play</u>?   Give
        an example of each.

    b. Define and give an example of <u>sensorimotor</u> play.

    c. Define <u>imaginative</u> <u>play</u> and briefly describe the five major
        types.

d. Briefly discuss the constructive role of imaginative play in contributing to the child's development of cognitive skills.

e. What is the relationship between having an imaginary playmate and later creativity? With what else is such a playmate cor-related?

f. Of what value may fairy tales be to development?

g. Define and give an example of social play.

h. Define and give an example of parallel play. How is it different from cooperative play?

i. Identify the three types of games described by Piaget.

j. Outline at least three sex differences in play.

8. Sex roles

    a. Distinguish between sex roles and sex typing.

    b. Briefly describe Mead's study of three New Guinea tribes. What did she conclude about masculinity and femininity?

    c. On what grounds has Mead's study been criticized? Briefly describe an alternative explanation of her observations.

9. Sex typing and sex roles

    a. Outline at least three sexual stereotypes for boys and three for girls.

    b. What forces are operating to change many of these stereotypes?

    c. What three forces appear to influence the development of sex roles? Give an example of each.

d. What four criteria must be met before one can begin to assert
    that a sex difference is genetically based? How do sex dif-
    ferences in aggressiveness stack up against these criteria?

e. What factors other than sex should be considered in an
    analysis of aggression?

f. What evidence is there to suggest that children can
    discriminate between masculine and feminine traits?

g. How do males and females differ, on the average, with respect
    to verbal facility, achievement motivation, spatial ability,
    mathematical skills aggression, and affiliation?

h. Briefly describe how parental attitudes affect sex roles.

i. Briefly describe sex differences reported in cross-cultural
    studies involving cultures vastly different from our own.

j. Explain what inferences you can make about a specific individual when you are confronted with a statement such as, "On the average, girls are less competitive than boys."

Multiple-Choice Posttest

1. Which of the following statements is correct? (a) A central question for child psychologists is determining which aspects of behavior are most affected by culture; (b) Culture is typically defined as the sum total of traditions, mores, beliefs, and attitudes that characterize a group of people; (c) It is logical to argue that those aspects of child behavior that are least variable from one culture to another result from hereditary influences; (d) All of the above are correct.

2. There is less pressure to conform in our society because: (a) anonymity provides respite from group pressure; (b) the pressure the group can bring to bear on the individual is remote; (c) there is no single code of approved conduct; (d) all of the above.

3. Asch's study of the effects of group pressure indicated that: (a) people who are strong-willed or well educated are less likely to conform to social pressures than people who are weak-willed or poorly educated; (b) people will frequently contradict their beliefs as a result of group pressure; (c) subjects will almost invariably agree with the majority, if the majority is large enough; (d) all of the above.

4. Which of the following statements is correct? (a) Minority groups in the United States and Canada are typically defined on the basis of personality and intellectual characteristics; (b) Research has shown that proportionately more socially disadvantaged children attend college than advantaged children, since disadvantaged children know they have more to overcome; (c) Socially advantaged children typically score higher on college entrance exams than disadvantaged children; (d) All of the above are correct.

139

5. Which of the following statements is correct? (a) Observational learning becomes less important and less prevalent as the complexity of the culture increases; (b) Social learning theory holds that culture is transmitted through a process of imitation; (c) Symbolic models are more prevalent in primitive cultures than in complex, technological ones; (d) All of the above are correct.

6. Which of the following statements is correct? (a) Language development is apparently harmed by TV viewing, particularly among children from low socioeconomic and minority groups; (b) Research has demonstrated that TV influences prosocial behavior as well as aggressive behavior; (c) The elderly spend more time watching TV than any other age group; (d) All of the above are correct.

7. Which of the following statements is correct? (a) Children who view prosocial programs tend to be more cooperative than children who view antisocial programs; (b) Children who watch TV typically read as many books as children who are nonviewers; (c) Preference for violent programs is positively correlated with aggressive and delinquent behavior; (d) All of the above are correct.

8. The (   ) hypothesis of TV influences argues that TV serves to trigger aggressive urges that were present prior to the program that motivated the act: (a) catalyst; (b) cathartic; (c) modeling; (d) no-effect.

9. Although Dan is not an aggressive person, he loves to watch violent TV programs, particularly ones that involve boxing. He says he loses all thoughts of being hostile by watching these programs. What hypothesis of TV influence best explains this example? (a) catalyst; (b) cathartic; (c) modeling; (d) no-effect.

10. (   ) play is evident in the countless solitary games young children play for the sheer sensations involved: (a) Imaginative; (b) Parallel; (c) Sensorimotor; (d) Social.

11. Pretending that you are Darth Vadar or Han Solo is a form of (   ) play: (a) imaginative; (b) manipulative; (c) sensorimotor; (d) social.

12. Which of the following statements is correct? (a) Children with imaginary playmates tend to be less aggressive and to view TV less than children who do not have such playmates; (b) Fairy tales may have a beneficial effect on development due to their symbolic nature; (c) Daydreaming may play a constructive role in the development of cognitive skills; (d) All of the above are correct.

13. (   ) play can be characterized as interaction between two or more children, the use of rules, and cooperation: (a) Imaginative; (b) Manipulative; (c) Sensorimotor; (d) Social.

14. The learning of sex-appropriate behavior is referred to as: (a) sex roling; (b) sex typing; (c) sexual stereotyping; (d) sexual differentiation.

15. Which of the following conditions would have to be met before one could begin to conclude that a sex role was genetically based? (a) It would not be manifest until environmental forces were present to modify it; (b) It would be present in only those cultures that have strong genetic predispositions; (c) It would probably be evident in subhuman primates; (d) All of the above.

16. Which of the following statements is correct? (a) Much research, including that with nonhuman primates, indicates that males are more aggressive than females; (b) There appears to be much widespread disagreement, at least among college students, in categorizing masculine and feminine traits; (c) Surprisingly, research has shown that parental attitudes appear to be of little importance in determining sex role behavior of children; (d) All of the above are correct.

17. On the average, boys (   ) than girls: (a) learn to read earlier; (b) are more aggressive; (c) show a higher need to affiliate; (d) all of the above.

18. Boys are typically considered to be (   ) than girls: (a) better at spatial-visual tasks; (b) better in mathematics; (c) more aggressive; (d) all of the above.

Answers to Posttest

1. d (p.291) 2. d (p.291) 3. b (p.291) 4. c (p.290) 5. b (p.293)
6. b (p.297) 7. d (p.297) 8. a (p.299) 9. b (p.299) 10. c (p.302)
11. a (p.302) 12. d (p.303) 13. d (p.306) 14. b (p.309) 15. c (p.311)
16. a (p.310) 17. b (p.312) 18. d (p.312)

CHAPTER 12:

COGNITIVE DEVELOPMENT IN MIDDLE CHILDHOOD

Introduction

The long interval between the end of the preschool period and adolescence is marked by continuing changes in all areas of development. These changes frequently do not appear to be as dramatic as those that occurred earlier, partly because many of them are quantitative rather than qualitative. For example, preschool children have already learned to walk, speak, and perhaps to reason, though somewhat inexpertly and illogically. In subsequent years they simply learn more words, refine their knowledge of grammar, acquire a great deal of specific information, learn to run more rapidly and to jump farther, and become larger. In addition, they become more socialized, achieve greater independence from their immediate family, place greater reliance on their peers, and change intellectually and morally.

Chapter 12 opens with a discussion of middle childhood theory that covers physical growth, intellectual development, intelligence, and creativity. The growth spurt--earlier for girls than for boys-- occurs near the top limit of middle childhood. The chapter then looks at cognitive development as described by Piaget, pausing to note that at the end of the period of concrete operations, the child is still tied to the "real" rather than to the hypothetical. Finally it examines intelligence--an imprecise and much abused concept--and creativity.

Key Terms and Concepts

1. Middle childhood (six to twelve years)
    Six: 46 inches; 48 pounds; 2,500 word vocabulary; syntax;
       intuitive thought; enters Freud's latency stage
    Twelve: 5 feet; 84-87 pounds; logic for concrete problems;
       symbolic thought; enters Freud's genital stage

2. Physical development
    Boys vs. girls in height and weight
    Fatty tissue decreases
    Growth spurt: earlier for girls than for boys

3. Motor development
     Fine muscle control improves
     Coordination and strength increase
     Sex differences
     Reaction time decreases

4. Intellectual development
     Concrete operations (Piaget)
     Thought becomes more logical
     Conservation
       Identity, reversibility, compensation
       Substance, length, numbers, liquids, area
       Extinction studies
     Acceleration of conservation
       Little generalization to other tasks
       Mixed success
     Other abilities
       Class inclusion: combining and decomposing classes
       Seriation
       Concept of numbers
     Thought is both concrete and operational

5. Intelligence
     What the tests test: a definition by Boring
     Validity and reliability
     Numerous definitions
     Misconceptions
       IQ is not a fixed quantity but a mathematical expression
       IQ is related to school success but not as much as to
         previous achievement
     Weaknesses
       Do not measure personality characteristics such as motivation
       Frequently culturally biased
       Widely used, though sometimes inappropriately

6. Measuring intelligence
     Stanford-Binet (individual test)
       IQ = MA/CA X 100
       Average (mean) = 100
     Wechsler (individual tests): independent measures of verbal
       and performance skills
     IQ constancy: increases with increasing age
     Piaget-based measures
       Little or no relation between Piagetian tasks and IQ
       Tasks are different and are based on different assumptions

7. Creativity
    Correlation with intelligence
    Convergent vs. divergent thinking
    Encouraging creativity: brainstorming

Short-Answer Questions

1. Middle childhood

    a. What is middle childhood? When does it typically begin?
        When does it typically end? How is its termination defined?

    b. Briefly compare six- and twelve-year-old children, both
        physically and behaviorally.

    c. Describe the transitions that mark the onset and termination
        of middle childhood as advanced by Freud and by Piaget. (Be
        sure to name the appropriate developmental stages in your
        description.)

2. Physical development

    a. In general, how do boys and girls differ in height, in
        weight, and in muscle development between the ages of six and
        twelve?

    b. What happens to the proportion of fatty tissue between ages
        six and twelve?

c. What is the <u>growth</u> <u>spurt</u>? How do boys and girls differ in terms of its onset?

3. <u>Motor</u> <u>development</u>

   a. Name at least two general changes that occur in motor ability between the ages of six and twelve.

   b. How do boys and girls differ on such tasks as standing-start jumps, long jumps, hopscotch, and throwing a ball? What general conclusions can be drawn from these findings?

   c. What is <u>reaction</u> <u>time</u>? How does a five-year-old child's reaction time compare with that of an adult? Explain the importance of reaction time in the development of the child's motor abilities.

4. <u>Intellectual</u> <u>development</u>

   a. What major stage of intellectual development is predominant during middle childhood? What marks the transition to this stage?

   b. Define <u>conservation</u>. Give two examples of a conservation task.

c. What are the three logical rules characteristic of a child's
    thinking at the stage of concrete operations? Define and
    give an example of each.

d. What are the five typical conservation tasks? At what age is
    each usually mastered?

e. Briefly cite the evidence that the rules of logic of the con-
    crete operational child are not completely general.

f. What general question do conservation-training experiments
    try to answer?   Generally, how successful have they been?
    Explain.

g. Conservation-training frequently does not generalize to other
    tasks.   Why is this important in interpreting results of
    conservation-training studies?

h. What is <u>class</u> <u>inclusion</u>? Give an example.

i. What is <u>seriation</u>? Give an example.

j. What two factors in a child's learning are important to an
understanding of numbers? Explain. How are these two factors related to the ordinal and cardinal properties of
numbers?

k. To summarize <u>concrete</u> <u>operations</u>, explain why a child's
logical operations during middle childhood are classified as
concrete. Give an example.

5. <u>Intelligence</u>

a. There are numerous definitions of <u>intelligence</u> but no general
agreement concerning what it is or how it should be measured.
Comment on the statement: Intelligence is what the tests
test.

b. Define <u>reliability</u> and <u>validity</u>.

c. Briefly comment on the following misconceptions about IQ: it
is a fixed entity possessed in lesser or greater quantities
by everyone; it is highly related to success.

d. Briefly comment on the following weaknesses of traditional
    measures of intelligence: absence of personality variables:

Measuring Intelligence

a. How are the Stanford-Binet and Wechsler tests administered?

b. Briefly describe the Stanford-Binet test.

c. What is the mathematical equation for computing IQ? Describe
    what MA and CA represent in this equation.

d. If a child is nine years old and can answer all the questions
    designed for ten-year-olds, what would the child's IQ be?

e. Draw and label the curve that represents the distribution of
    IQ scores. (Be sure to indicate the mean and standard devia-
    tion.)

f.   How do the Wechsler tests differ from the Stanford-Binet?

g.   [illegible] What evidence is there to support your assertion?

h.   How do intelligence scales paralleling Piaget's descriptions of cognitive development correlate with other, more traditional intelligence test scales? Speculate about why such a correlation may exist.

7.   Creativity

   a.   What is the relation between creativity and intelligence? What factors might account for this relationship?

   b.   How is creativity frequently measured? Give an example.

   c.   What is the difference between divergent and convergent thinking? Give an example of each.

149

d. Define brainstorming. Give an example that illustrates how this procedure can be used.

Multiple-Choice Posttest

1. Middle childhood begins: (a) at age six and ends at about age twelve; (b) with the onset of puberty; (c) with the transition from concrete to formal operational thought; (d) all of the above.

2. The average twelve-year-old: (a) is in the phallic stage of psychosexual development (Freud); (b) is nearly four feet tall; (c) weighs about 84 pounds; (d) all of the above.

3. During middle childhood: (a) boys are typically more interested than girls in muscular activity; (b) girls are initially shorter and lighter than boys; (c) girls go through a growth spurt two years earlier than boys; (d) all of the above.

4. Which of the following statements is correct? (a) A five-year-old's reaction time is twice as long as that of an adult; (b) During middle childhood, the child is in Freud's phallic stage of psychosexual development; (c) Middle childhood begins with the transition from sensorimotor to preoperational thought; (d) All of the above are correct.

5. The predominant intellectual stage during middle childhood according to Piaget is: (a) sensorimotor; (b) preoperational; (c) formal operational; (d) concrete operations.

6. The acquisition of concepts of conservation is evidence that the child: (a) can make use of certain laws of logic including identity, reversibility, and compensation; (b) has progressed from preoperational thinking to the stage of concrete operations; (c) realizes that characteristics of a substance such as weight, volume, and area do not change in spite of misleading perceptual changes in their appearance; (d) all of the above.

7. Piaget defines conservation as the realization that:
    (a) activities can be undone mentally; (b) adding two quantities
    yields a third distinct quantity; (c) the quantitative aspects
    of objects do not change unless something is added or removed;
    (d) all of the above.

8. Children who answer a conservation-of-mass problem correctly
    would be reasoning using the law of identity if they say: (a) it
    can never be changed back to what it was; (b) it only appears
    larger; (c) nothing has been added or taken away; (d) they can
    identify the new mass.

9. A logical law specifying that several operations can be combined
    in several ways to yield the same result refers to Piaget's con-
    cept of: (a) compensation; (b) identity; (c) object per-
    manence; (d) reversibility.

10. According to Piaget, which of the following types of conservation
    appears last? (a) area; (b) length; (c) liquids; (d) number.

11. Evidence that the concrete operational child's rules of logic are
    not completely general is derived from studies in which the child
    is actually deceived by the experimenter and then asked to
    justify his or her logic. These are referred to as (   )
    studies. (a) acceleration; (b) compensation; (c) extinction;
    (d) reversibility.

12. The results of several studies designed to accelerate conserva-
    tion suggest that: (a) children learn an empirical rule during
    training but have not acquired the logical understanding of the
    tasks; (b) responding appropriately to conservation tasks cannot
    be learned until the child has entered the stage of formal
    operational thinking; (c) when conservation on one task is
    learned, it will frequently generalize to other tasks; (d) all of
    the above.

13. When shown one robin, two sparrows, and five ducks and asked,
    "Are there more birds or ducks?" a child responds, "More birds."
    The child is in this example demonstrating: (a) class inclusion;
    (b) egocentric thought; (c) intuitive thinking; (d) seriation.

14. Which of the following statements is correct? (a) In order to
    understand classification, the child must be able to understand
    numbers and to seriate; (b) In order to understand numbers, the
    child must be able to classify and to think propositionally;
    (c) In order to understand numbers, the child must be able to
    classify and to seriate; (d) In order to understand seriation,
    the child must be able to deal with numbers and to classify.

15. Which of the following statements is correct? (a) IQ is a fixed entity possessed in lesser or greater quantities by everyone; (b) Success in school is related more to a person's IQ than it is to his or her previous achievements; (c) There are numerous definitions of intelligence, and controversy still exists about whether it is a single quality or a number of separate abilities; (d) All of the above are correct.

16. If Henry's mental age exceeds his chronological age, his IQ will be: (a) equal to 100; (b) less than 100; (c) greater than 100; (d) impossible to determine, since not enough information is provided.

17. John has a mental age of 6 and an IQ of 80. How old is he? (a) 4.8 years; (b) 7.5 years; (c) 9.6 years; (d) 13.3 years.

18. Which of the following statements is correct? (a) Constancy of IQ scores decreases with increasing age; (b) IQ is relatively constant, but due to individual variations, one should be cautious of their predictability; (c) IQ scores of most infants are accurate predictions of later IQ scores; (d) All of the above are correct.

19. (   ) thinking is to an aptitude test as (   ) thinking is to a test of creativity: (a) Concrete operational; formal operational; (b) Convergent; divergent; (c) Divergent; convergent; (d) Formal operational; concrete operational.

20. Brainstorming is a technique that: (a) attempts to have members of the group reach consensus about the best possible solution to a problem; (b) promotes divergent thinking; (c) requires members of the group to evaluate ideas presented by others; (d) all of the above.

Answers to Posttest

1. a (p.318) 2. c (p.319) 3. d (p.320) 4. a (p.323) 5. d (p.324)
6. d (p.325) 7. c (p.325) 8. c (p.325) 9. a (p.325) 10. a (p.327)
11. c (p.326) 12. a (p.328) 13. a (p.329) 14. c (p.330) 15. c (p.332)
16. c (p.334) 17. b (p.334) 18. b (p.335) 19. b (p.337) 20. b (p.337)

CHAPTER 13:

SOCIAL DEVELOPMENT IN MIDDLE CHILDHOOD

Introduction

From middle childhood through adolescence, the influences on a child's social development shift from family and early cultural environment to peer groups and school. Chapter 13 relates these new socializing influences to the development of morality as reflected by specific prosocial and antisocial behaviors. Research in this area indicates that empathy and caring, high levels of moral orientation, and prosocial behavior are closely correlated.

Key Terms and Concepts

1. Peer groups
   Changes in influence between ages six and twelve
   Characteristics of peer groups during middle childhood
     Like-sexed, loose-knit
     Prado's dart-throwing experiment: shifting allegiances
   Influence of deprivation from peers on monkeys
   Peer acceptance and rejection
     Well-liked children: friendly and sociable
   Sociometry: technique for assessing peer relations
   Friendship patterns
     Most children have several close friends, not just one
     Girls are more intimate and cooperative
   Functions of peer groups
     Self-concept
     Sexual attitudes and behaviors

2. The school
   Basic skills and knowledge
   Minority groups
   Teacher expectations may have an effect
     Results of studies are contradictory
     Rosenthal effect
   Self-expectations: attribution theory
     The way people assign responsibility for success and failure
     Internally oriented (mastery); externally oriented (helpless)
     Mastery: achievement oriented, feelings of being capable
     Helplessness: learned

3. Childhood morality
    Kohlberg's three aspects of morality
       Resisting temptation
       Guilt that accompanies failure to resist temptation
       Estimate of morality based on good and evil
    Conscience
       Freud's superego: not supported by research
       Religious model: no correlation between overt behavior and
          religious training
       Moral behavior seems to be a function of will (ego-strength),
          a decision-making capacity

4. Moral development
    Internalization of rules
    Three stages in rule-governed behavior
       Prior to age three, no understanding
       Next, rules derived from external sources
       Finally, rules are made by people and can be changed
    Relation between cheating and chance of getting caught
    Two stages in evolution of guilt or culpability
       Prior to age nine or ten, objective consequences of the act
          are most important
       After ten, consideration of motives behind the act
    Social learning: imitation and reinforcement/punishment
    Kohlberg's stages
       Premoral stage: subjective consequences and hedonism
       Morality of conventional role conformity: conformance to
          rules to gain approval or in response to authority
       Morality of self-accepted principles: conscience and
          individual rights
       Kohlberg's stages have been seriously questioned
    Implications of research on moral development
       Relation to delinquency
       Parental model
       Caring for others

5. Prosocial behavior
    Can be fostered through the use of models
    Cooperative play increases with age, as does competitiveness
    Social class and cultural differences
    Role-taking: emotional and cognitive
    Empathy: fundamental to development of altruism

6. Antisocial behaviors such as aggression
    Psychological explanation: consequence of frustration
    Ethological: response to biological predispositions
    Social learning: attributable to models
    Physiological: hormones and brain structure
    Sex differences

Short-Answer Questions

1. Peer groups

    a. What is a peer group? Identify two such groups to which you belong.

    b. Name two characteristics of peer groups during middle child-hood.

    c. When do peers begin to become particularly important as socializing agents in the child's life? Why do you suppose the transition occurs at this time?

    d. How does Prado's dart-throwing experiment illustrate a shift in the child's allegiance between middle childhood and adolescence?

    e. What does the evidence from studies of monkeys reared in isolation suggest about the importance of peers?

    f. Name four factors that appear to lead to peer acceptance.

    g. What is sociometry? What is a sociogram? Give an example of the latter.

h. How many close friends do most children have? How do boys and girls differ with respect to the amount of intimacy and cooperativeness in their friendships?

i. How are self-concept and popularity related? Give an example.

j. Explain the importance of peer groups in the formation of sexually appropriate values and attitudes.

k. What is the relationship between how long someone has been a member of a group and his or her values?

2. The school

a. Identify two important functions of school.

b. Name at least three reasons why children from minority groups have a rougher time in public school than children from the more advantaged majority.

c. Briefly describe the Rosenthal and Jacobson studies of teacher expectations. How were the subjects selected? What were the results? On what grounds have the studies been criticized?

d. Explain how teacher expectations might <u>lower</u> the achievement level of minority-group children. Can you think of a way to alleviate this problem?

e. What is <u>attribution theory</u>?

f. Explain how attribution theory differentiates between externally and internally motivated people. Cite at least two differences in how children in each class behave.

3. <u>Childhood morality</u>

a. What are Kohlberg's three aspects of morality?

b. Briefly describe the two classical approaches to analysis of a strong conscience. What evidence exists to support each approach?

c. What does Kohlberg mean when he says that moral behavior is a matter of strength of will (ego strength)?

4. <u>Moral development</u>

a. According to Piaget, how are <u>morality</u> and <u>understanding</u> <u>of</u> <u>rules</u> related?

b. Briefly describe the three stages that a child goes through in understanding the rules of a game. Be sure to indicate the ages at which transitions are made.

c. According to Hartshorne and May, to what is cheating primarily related?

d. Briefly characterize the two broad stages in the evolution of a child's beliefs about culpability (guilt). When does the transition between them typically occur?

e. Briefly describe how social learning theory explains the acquisition of rules.

f.   What are the three levels of morality, according to Kohlberg?
     Briefly describe and give an example of each.

g.   According to Kohlberg, what are the two predominant charac-
     teristics of moral development during middle childhood? Give
     an example of each.

h.   On what grounds have Kohlberg's stages been challenged?

i.   Briefly describe the implications of research on moral
     development in each of the following areas:

     delinquency -

     parental models -

     caring for others -

5. Prosocial behavior

    a.   Briefly describe the Paulson study on the effects of models
         on cooperative behavior. What were the results?

b. Briefly discuss the relationship between the following:

sex differences and cooperative behavior -

age and cooperation -

age and rivalry -

cultural differences and prosocial behavior -

c. Define role-taking and briefly describe what research has shown about its development.

d. Define empathy. Why is it difficult to study? How does its development progress in comparison to role-taking?

6. Antisocial behaviors

a. Briefly describe each of the following explanations of aggression:

frustration -

ethological -

social learning -

physiological -

b. How do males and females differ in terms of aggressiveness?

c. What is the current emphasis of research on antisocial behavior?

Multiple-Choice Posttest

1. The results of Prado's dart-throwing experiment indicate that: (a) children who are friendly and sociable tend to be more easily accepted than those who are hostile and unsociable; (b) children who are well-liked tend to have favorable self-concepts; (c) there is a marked increase in the importance of peers during middle childhood; (d) all of the above.

2. Which of the following statements is correct? (a) Studies of monkeys reared in isolation indicate that isolated monkeys are frequently retarded in their subsequent social development; (b) Most Canadian and American children belong to no more than one peer group; (c) Peers begin to replace the family as a socializing agent about the age of 9 or 10; (d) All of the above are correct.

3. Which of the following statements is correct? (a) Children who have several close peers typically have a low self-concept since their values and attitudes are defined more by the group than by themselves; (b) Most children in middle childhood have one "best" friend, someone with whom they share most activities; (c) Peer groups in middle childhood typically consist of like-sex children of approximately the same age; (d) All of the above are correct.

161

4. Which of the following statements is correct? (a) Girls are typically more cooperative with one another during middle childhood than are boys; (b) Girls typically have more close friends during middle childhood than boys; (c) In competitive situations during middle childhood, when doing best means losing out personally, close friends typically behave altruistically; (d) All of the above are correct.

5. Research indicates that sociability and acceptance are: (a) unrelated; (b) positively correlated; (c) negatively correlated; (d) related, but only for children from low socioeconomic groups.

6. The longer one is a member of a peer group: (a) the greater the diversity of values and attitudes to which they are exposed; (b) the less diverse their values are from the group's; (c) the less group values actually influence behavior; (d) all of the above.

7. One of the dependent variables in the Rosenthal and Jacobson study of teacher expectations was: (a) the child's grade level in school; (b) the child's performance on IQ tests; (c) the instructions given to the teachers; (d) whether or not the child was identified as a bloomer.

8. Internally oriented (mastery oriented) children: (a) are likely to attribute success to ability or effort; (b) see themselves as capable even when they fail; (c) tend to be highly achievement oriented; (d) all of the above.

9. Which of the following is not one of the three aspects of morality according to Kohlberg? (a) amount of guilt that accompanies failure to resist temptation; (b) behavioral aspects of morality, reflected in a person's ability to resist temptation; (c) the individual's estimate of morality of a given act, based on some personal standard of good or evil; (d) the stronger a person's belief about the immorality of an act, the less likely he or she is to engage in that act.

10. Piaget defines morality as: (a) a concrete operation; (b) internalization of rules; (c) symbolization of culpability; (d) all of the above.

11. According to Piaget, which of the following statements is correct? (a) A child has no adherence to rules until approximately age three; (b) Between the ages three and five, children imitate rules but do not really understand them; (c) Not until eleven or twelve does a child realize that rules exist to make games possible and that they can be altered by mutual agreement; (d) All of the above are correct.

12. Kohlberg's analysis of the development of morality in children indicates that it occurs in the following order: (a) hedonism, response to authority, self-accepted principles; (b) response to authority, hedonism, self-accepted principles; (c) response to authority, self-accepted principles, hedonism; (d) self-accepted principles, response to authority, hedonism.

13. Morality defined in terms of individual rights (Kohlberg) is predominant during: (a) infancy; (b) the preschool years; (c) middle childhood; (d) adolescence.

14. Which of the following statements is correct? (a) During early and middle childhood, doing what is considered right is highly influenced by the chances of getting caught; (b) In terms of Kohlberg's stages of moral development, one of the highest levels of attainment is acting in terms of accepted conventions; (c) Research has demonstrated that there is a very close relationship between beliefs and behavior; (d) All of the above are correct.

15. Which of the following statements is correct? (a) Caring for others appears to be an important factor in fostering progression from lower to higher levels of morality; (b) Children who operate at the hedonistic level of moral development are more likely to be delinquent than those who have self-accepted principles of conscience; (c) Most studies of Kohlberg's stages of moral development have not confirmed either the order or ages at which children go through the various stages; (d) All of the above are correct.

16. (   ) is to emotional development as (   ) is to cognitive development: (a) Altruism; egocentricity; (b) Egocentricity; altruism; (c) Empathy; role-taking; (d) Role-taking; empathy.

17. The (   ) explanation of aggression argues that aggression results from biological predispositions: (a) ethological; (b) frustration; (c) physiological; (d) social learning theory.

Answers to Posttest

1. c (p.343) 2. a (p.344) 3. c (p.342) 4. a (p.347) 5. b (p.347)
6. b (p.348) 7. b (p.350) 8. d (p.351) 9. d (p.352) 10. b (p.353)
11. d (p.354) 12. a (p.355) 13. d (p.356) 14. a (p.355) 15. d (p.358)
16. c (p.362) 17. a (p.363)

CHAPTER 14:

EXCEPTIONAL CHILDREN

Introduction

Chapter 14 addresses exceptionality, taking care to point out that just as some individuals are exceptionally handicapped, so too are some exceptionally advantaged. It takes up in turn physical, social/emotional, and intellectual exceptionality, and for each case it discusses prevalence, possible causes, manifestations, and special services. We have yet to display as great a recognition of our responsibilities toward the gifted as we do toward the disadvantaged. In conclusion, the chapter examines some important trends in special education--deinstitutionalization and mainstreaming--and the controversies associated with each.

Key Terms and Concepts

1. Exceptionality
   Two kinds: gifted and disadvantaged
   Dimensions: physical, social/emotional, and cognitive
   A definition of those who require special help to realize
      their full potential
   Who needs what services
   Labels

2. Physical exceptionality
   Nonsensory
      Many are congenital
      Cerebral palsy
      Epilepsy
      Other physical problems
   Visual impairment
   Hearing impairment: most often congenital
      More serious than visual problems
      Related to language development
      Manual vs. oral approach to teaching language
   Physically gifted children

3. Social-emotional exceptionality
        Frequently difficult to identify
            Labels are not explanations
            From 2 percent to 20 percent of the school population
            Predisposing vs. precipitating causes
            Biogenic vs. psychogenic factors
        Autism and schizophrenia: institutional care
        Hyperkinesis
            Genetic component: twin studies and sex differences
            Maturational component
            Frequently treated with drugs
        Conduct and personality disorders
        Social-emotional giftedness
            Invulnerables: exceptionally competent socially
            Exposure to some adversity may be important

4. Intellectual exceptionality
        Mental retardation: inability to learn
            IQ performance
            Profound, severe, moderate, mild
            Custodial, trainable, educable
        Mild or educable mentally retarded (IQs 50-70): 75 percent
        Severe to moderate or trainable (IQs 25-50): 20 percent
        Severe or custodial (IQs 0-25): 5 percent
        Education of the mildly retarded
            Do not learn differently from others
            Short-term memory deficiencies
            Some language and motor difficulties
        Learning disabilities
            Performance below expectation
            Wide range of learning problems
            Difficult to define and identify
        Intellectual giftedness
            Intelligence: IQ test scores
            Creativity
            High task orientation

5. Trends and controversies in special education
        Deinstitutionalization and nonsegregation (public schools)
        Mainstreaming: regular classrooms
            Effects mixed
        Labels
            Negative effects: expectations and self-concept
            Sometimes convenient, if used judiciously

Short-Answer Questions

1. <u>Exceptionality</u>

    a. What are the two types of exceptional individuals?

    b. What are the three dimensions of exceptionality?

    c. There is general agreement that exceptional children include those who require special education and services to realize their full potential. If the problem is not the definition, what is it?

    d. Briefly discuss the pros and cons of the use of labels and classification systems.

2. <u>Physical exceptionality</u>

    The physically gifted may include wine tasters and perfume smellers, but individuals with these abilities do not typically receive much special service in our culture.

    a. What three types of physical exceptionality does the text consider?

    b. What is a <u>congenital defect</u>? Give two examples.

c. Briefly describe <u>cerebral</u> <u>palsy</u> and name three congenital factors associated with it.

d. Briefly characterize <u>epilepsy</u>.

e. Name four other physical problems that would be considered "exceptional."

f. Why is the term <u>visually impaired</u> preferable to <u>blind</u>?

g. What is the difference between <u>prelinguistic</u> and <u>postlinguistic</u> deafness? Which occurs most frequently? Why is the distinction an important one?

h. Why are hearing impairments considered more serious than visual impairments? Cite at least two reasons.

i. Briefly describe the two major approaches to teaching language to the deaf.

3. <u>Social/emotional</u> <u>exceptionality</u>

    a. Why is social/emotional exceptionality difficult to identify?

    b. Distinguish between <u>predisposing</u> and <u>precipitating</u> causes.

    c. Distinguish between <u>biogenic</u> and <u>psychogenic</u> factors.

    d. Briefly characterize <u>autism</u>. What type of care does it typically require?

    e. Briefly characterize childhood <u>schizophrenia</u>.

    f. Define <u>hyperkinesis</u>. Identify two sources of information that suggest it has a genetic component. What evidence is there that it has a maturational component? How is it frequently treated?

    g. Name six common conduct and personality disorders.

h. Briefly characterize children who are labeled <u>invulnerable</u> in terms of their history of emotional disorders and typical behavior.

i. Why does Anthony believe some adversity may be crucial for development?

4. <u>Intellectual exceptionality</u>

    a. Define <u>mental retardation</u>. How is it typically measured?

    b. Compare the two major systems for classifying mental retardation.

    c. Identify four potential causes of mental retardation.

    d. What percent of retarded individuals are only mildly or educably mentally retarded (EMR)? What IQ range does this category encompass? Typically, where are these individuals first detected?

e. What percent of retarded individuals are moderately to severely retarded (trainable)? What IQ range does this category span? What kind of care is typically provided?

f. What percent are severely or profoundly retarded? What IQ range does this category span? What kind of care is typically provided?

g. To what extent is learning different for mildly retarded children than for normal children? How do these two groups differ with respect to memory and attention span? Identify two other areas in which mildly retarded children may sometimes be deficient.

h. Name five common learning disabilities. How is learning disability typically defined? Why are these disabilities difficult to define and identify?

i. List three methods by which the intellectually gifted are frequently identified.

j. What kinds of programs are available for the intellectually gifted? Why do you suppose society places more emphasis on the disadvantaged than on the gifted?

5. Trends and controversies in special education

    a. What is the current trend in the treatment of exceptional children? What have been the consequences of this trend?

    b. Define mainstreaming. How effective has it been as a procedure for dealing with mildly retarded children?

    c. Briefly describe the case against the use of labels. Do labels appear to have any value?

Multiple-Choice Posttest

1. Which of the following is not typically considered a dimension of exceptionality?   (a) cognitive;   (b) personal;   (c) physical; (d) social/emotional.

2. Which of the following statements is correct?   (a) A major problem in special education is determining who needs special education and what services will be optimal for them; (b) Exceptional children are defined as those who need special education and services to realize their full potential;   (c) One reason many people react negatively to the use of labels is because educators have too often adjusted their expectations and behavior unfairly in reaction to those labels;   (d) All of the above are correct.

171

3. The physical syndrome that includes motor problems, psychological problems, convulsions, and behavior disorders is called: (a) autism, (b) cerebral palsy; (c) epilepsy; (d) hyperkinesis.

4. Which of the following statements is correct? (a) Deafness is generally more serious if it occurs prior to the age of two than if it occurs after the age of two; (b) Most people who are classified as visually impaired cannot see anything but changes in illumination; (c) Research has clearly established that the oral approach is superior to the manual approach for teaching language to deaf children; (d) All of the above are correct.

5. The ( ) approach to teaching language to deaf people involves gestures and includes such techniques as American Sign Language and fingerspelling: (a) manual; (b) prelinguistic; (c) postlinguistic; (d) oral.

6. Which of the following statements is correct? (a) Hearing is more important than vision in the acquisition of language; (b) Labels such as autism only serve to describe social and emotional problems; they do not explain these behaviors and symptoms; (c) Social/emotional exceptionalities are relatively difficult to define and classify; (d) All of the above are correct.

7. ( ) factors in the development of emotional disturbances include genetic and biological forces whereas ( ) factors are related to the child's relationship with the environment: (a) Biogenic; psychogenic; (b) Predisposing; precipitating; (c) Precipitating; predisposing; (d) Psychogenic; biogenic.

8. Which of the following would probably not be classified as a social/ emotional disturbance? (a) aggressiveness; (b) autism; (c) hostility; (d) mental retardation.

9. Which of the following statements is correct? (a) If one member of a pair of twins is hyperactive, the other has a high probability of not being hyperactive; (b) More males are hyperkinetic than females; (c) If (b) is correct, it provides evidence that hyperkinesis has a significant environmental component; (d) All of the above are correct.

10. Which of the following would probably not be classified as a conduct or personality disorder? (a) aggressiveness; (b) cerebral palsy; (c) social isolation; (d) stealing.

11. Which of the following statements is correct? (a) Even small amounts of adversity appear to retard the child's development of resistance to disturbance; (b) Invulnerables are typically exceptionally competent and at ease socially, highly autonomous,

and achievement oriented; (c) The biological and emotional backgrounds of invulnerables appears to be no different from the background of normal children; (d) All of the above are correct.

12. Which of the following statements is correct? (a) In practice, mental retardation is most often identified and defined in terms of its causes; (b) Most instances of mental retardation are due to brain damage and/or hereditary factors; (c) The most obvious feature of mental retardation is a general depression in ability to learn; (d) All of the above are correct.

13. Which of the following categories has the largest proportion of mentally retarded children? (a) custodial; (b) educable; (c) profoundly retarded; (d) trainable.

14. A child with an IQ of 12 would be classified as: (a) custodial; (b) educable; (c) moderately retarded; (d) trainable.

15. Which of the following statements is correct? (a) Children who are mildly retarded appear to have long-term memories comparable to normal children but are deficient in short-term memory and attending skills; (b) Children who are mildly retarded not only learn differently from normal children but also learn at a slower rate; (c) Mildly retarded children frequently are compensated for their deficiency by superior language facility or advanced motor skills; (d) All of the above are correct.

16. High (   ) would probably not be used to label an individual as intellectually gifted: (a) ability; (b) creativity; (c) invulnerability; (d) task commitment.

17. Which of the following statements is correct? (a) Critics of the use of labels argue that labels frequently alter expectations others have for the child and that they adversely affect the child's self-concept; (b) Mainstreaming involves placing exceptional children who otherwise would be placed in special classrooms in regular classrooms; (c) Studies of the effects of mainstreaming have produced conflicting results; (d) All of the above are correct.

Answers to Posttest

1. b (p.370) 2. d (p.371) 3. b (p.372) 4. a (p.374) 5. a (p.375)
6. d (p.374) 7. a (p.377) 8. d (p.376) 9. b (p.380) 10. b (p.380)
11. b (p.381) 12. c (p.383) 13. b (p.383) 14. a (p.383) 15. a (p.385)
16. c (p.386) 17. d (p.388)

CHAPTER 15:

ADOLESCENCE

Introduction

There has been considerable debate over whether adolescence is a general developmental phenomenon or whether it is peculiar to contemporary civilization--particularly Western societies. The problem remains unresolved, although it has been noted that in cultures exhibiting a clear demarcation between childhood and adulthood, children tend not to go through the turbulent period of adolescence. Our culture either does not demarcate passage to adulthood or contradicts itself when it does. To further confuse the issue, contemporary life styles demand long periods of economic unemployment while young adults prepare themselves for a career or while they are simply deciding what they should be if and when they grow up. Thus, we have adolescence, a sometimes troubled, stressful, and unpleasant stage of development.

Chapter 15 discusses first the physical changes that define adolescence--the period of transition between childhood and adulthood. It covers pubescence, the period in which the changes occur, and puberty, the consequent sexual maturity that follows pubescence. From a consideration of these momentous physical changes, the discussion turns to the social development of adolescents and an examination of the stages of socialization, from initial dependence on parents to relative independence. This change is greatly facilitated by interactions with peers, because peer groups have become central to the life of the adolescent.

The chapter next offers several profound observations about the subject of sex: sex exists; it is of considerable importance to the adolescent; masturbation is almost universal among males; 10 percent of all women never achieve orgasm; college students sometimes have intercourse; and early marriages are more likely to dissolve than later ones. From this topic, the chapter turns to the adolescent mind, contrasting it with the cognitive powers of middle childhood. The ability of adolescents to deal with the hypothetical, the logical nature of their thinking, and their idealism are discussed. Finally, the chapter examines three areas of turmoil: rebellion, drugs, and suicide. Some, though not all, students rebel; some, though not all, try drugs; relatively few choose to leave it all behind.

Key Terms and Concepts

1. The passage
    Frequently turbulent
    Continuous and discontinuous cultures

2. Physical changes
    Age of adolescence
    Puberty, pubescence, and menarch
    Age of sexual maturity: boys vs. girls
    Height, weight, and reach
    Concern about personal appearance
    Early vs. late sexual maturity: sexual differences

3. Social development: an overview
    Three general stages: dependence, conflict, independence
    Generation gap

4. Peers become increasingly important
    From isolated unisexual cliques to groups of couples
    Being well liked and liking others
    Low and high peer status (Gronlund and Holmlund)

5. Sex
    Changes in sexual beliefs and recent research
    Masturbation: common among adolescents
    Surveys of premarital sexual behavior hard to interpret
    Adolescent marriages: not likely to last
    Homosexuality: little activity among adolescents

6. Personality, self, and identity
    Understanding of self (Rogers)
    Erikson: identity crisis
    Self-esteem: peer relations, social class, parents

7. Intellectual development
    Inhelder and Piaget's test-tube task
    From concrete to formal operations
    Propositional thinking
    Many individuals do not learn how to think formally
    Idealism and formal operational thought

8. Turmoil topics
    Frustration: roles and ideals
    Delinquency: social class, peers, fathers, self-esteem
    Rebellion: popular stereotypes
    Drugs: marijuana, LSD, and many more
    Suicide: sex differences and college

1. The passage

    a. Why is adolescence frequently considered the most troubled period of child development?

    b. What is the difference between a continuous and a discontinuous culture? Which one is yours? Explain.

2. Physical changes

    a. What marks the onset of adolescence? At what age does this period typically end?

    b. Why is it difficult to define precisely when puberty occurs? How is it usually defined in girls? When does a girl typically become fertile? Explain.

    c. At what age does puberty typically begin in males? In females? Does it occur before, during, or after the growth spurt?

    d. How has the age of puberty (particularly in girls) been changing over the past few decades?

e. How consistent is the age of sexual maturity across different cultures?

f. What is <u>pubescence</u>? Identify two signs of pubescence in males and two in females.

g. Briefly compare changes in height and weight for males and females between the ages of twelve and eighteen.

h. Name two common worries of tenth-grade boys and two of tenth-grade girls. From your own experiences, are they accurate?

i. Briefly discuss the effects of early and late maturity on boys and on girls.

3. <u>Social development</u>. Briefly identify and describe the three stages of socialization during adolescence.

4. Importance of peer groups

   a. Name two outcomes that may occur if a child is isolated from his or her peers.

   b. Explain how, according to Dunphy, interactions with peers change between early and late adolescence.

   c. What is the relationship between liking others and being liked? Name two common characteristics of a well-liked child and two of a not-so-well-liked child.

   d. Briefly describe the Gronlund and Holmlund study of high and low peer status. What did the results indicate?

   e. Why is it not legitimate to conclude from the results of the Gronlund and Holmlund study that peer rejection causes school dropouts?

5. Sex

   a. How have sexual attitudes supposedly changed in recent generations? Briefly cite recent changes in the frequency of premarital sex among both males and females.

b. What is the most common form of sexual outlet for adoles-
    cents? How common is it? If done to excess, will it cause
    mental retardation or warts?

c. Briefly summarize the results of the Psychology Today survey
    of sexual patterns. How accurate do you think they are?
    Why?

d. How common is homosexuality among adolescents? How well is
    it accepted by adolescents?

e. How does the breakup rate in adolescent marriages compare
    with that in the general population? Why do you think this
    is so?

6. Personality, self, and identity

    a. Briefly, what is the self?

    b. According to Erikson, what is the primary developmental
        crisis facing the adolescent? How is it typically resolved?

    c. What is self-esteem, according to Coopersmith?

d. Name at least two things that are correlated with high self-esteem.

e. What is the relationship between social class and self-esteem?

f. What are the relationships among parental characteristics, child-rearing modes, and self-esteem?

7. Intellectual development

    a. What stage of intellectual development (Piaget) emerges in many children during their adolescent years?

    b. Consider the Inhelder and Piaget task involving the test tubes. Discuss how ten-year-olds differ from fourteen-year-olds in their solutions of the problem.

    c. How is propositional thinking different from concrete operational thought? Give an example of each.

    d. How is the adolescent's ability to deal with propositions important in formal operational thought? (Be sure you know what a proposition is.)

e. Give two reasons to explain why many adolescents and adults do not achieve Piaget's level of formal operational thought.

f. What is <u>idealism</u>? Give an example. How is it related to <u>formal operational</u> thought?

8. <u>Turmoil topics</u>

a. What are two principal sources of adolescent frustration? Give an example of each.

b. How does the adolescent react to society's demand for conformity? Explain why this frequently appears somewhat paradoxical.

c. How are <u>delinquents</u> typically defined? How is this definition limited? Explain.

d. Briefly discuss the relationship between delinquency and the following:

social class -

peer group -

fathers -

self-esteem -

sex of the delinquent -

e. How frequently does the social activist (rebel) fit the stereotype parents often describe? Give an example.

f. What are stereotypes? What are their major weaknesses?

g. What was so remarkable about the Stonies' discovery of digitalis?

h. Why does Lefrancois think that most estimates of drug use are too low?

i. Is marijuana addictive? What evidence is there to support the notion that smoking marijuana is the first step toward heroin addiction?

j. What is <u>LSD</u>? Name two of its more commonly noted effects. Are these effects consistent across individuals?

k. Briefly describe the relationship between age and suicide. Do more males or females commit suicide? Can you cite one or two possible reasons why this might be so?

l. Name two reasons why college students commit suicide. Why do you suppose college students are twice as likely to commit suicide as their noncollege counterparts?

Multiple-Choice Posttest

1. A discontinuous culture (as opposed to a continuous culture) is defined as one in which: (a) becoming an adult depends primarily on behaving as adults are permitted to behave; (b) mores, traditions, and beliefs are constantly transmitted from one generation to the next; (c) there are clear demarcations between various developmental stages; (d) all of the above.

2. Which of the following statements is correct? (a) Adolescence is universal in terms of the biological changes that accompany it; (b) A continuous culture is one in which there are clear demarcations between life stages; (c) The psychological implications of adolescence are highly consistent across different cultures; (d) All of the above are correct.

3. The term "puberty" refers primarily to: (a) changes that occur in late childhood or early adolescence; (b) resolution of the identity crisis; (c) sexual maturity; (d) stages in the development of sexual relations.

4. The occurrence of a girl's first menstrual period is termed: (a) menarche; (b) menopause; (c) meiosis; (d) mitosis.

5. Which of the following statements is correct? (a) Girls typically mature sexually before boys; (b) Menarche refers to the time between the girls first menstrual period and when she actually becomes fertile; (c) The age of the first menstrual period appears to be constant across generations and across cultures; (d) The growth spurt follows puberty by approximately two years.

6. Puberty: (a) occurs earlier in boys than in girls; (b) precedes the growth spurt; (c) is easier to define in girls than in boys; (d) all of the above.

7. Which of the following statements is correct? (a) At the age of twelve, boys are taller and heavier than girls; (b) Boys who mature early have more psychological problems than boys who mature later; (c) The average age for sexual maturity is twelve for girls and fourteen for boys; (d) All of the above are correct.

8. The period of adolescence: (a) has clearly demarcated boundaries in our culture; (b) is characterized by increasing degrees of dependence on parents; (c) is typically a period of conflict; (d) all of the above.

9. Late adolescence is characterized by: (a) heterosexual crowds; (b) heterosexual couples; (c) single-sex cliques; (d) single-sex crowds.

10. Which of the following statements is correct? (a) Adolescent marriages are more likely to end in divorce than marriages in the general population; (b) Most adolescents worry more about academic success than they do about their appearance; (c) Recent research indicates that homosexuality is common among adolescents; (d) All of the above are correct.

11. Data concerning sexual beliefs and behavior among adolescents indicate that: (a) homosexuality is a common occurrence among adolescents; (b) premarital sex is more prevalent than marital sex; (c) recent generations view themselves as more liberated sexually; (d) all of the above.

12. Which of the following statements is correct? (a) According to Erikson, the primary developmental crisis of the adolescent is to establish his or her identity; (b) Parental self-esteem is correlated with the self-esteem of their children; (c) Self-esteem is a personal judgment of worthiness that an individual holds of himself or herself; (d) All of the above are correct.

13. High self-esteem is correlated with: (a) adjustment; (b) achievement; (c) happiness; (d) all of the above.

14. The transition in logic from real and concrete to hypothetical marks the onset of Piaget's ( ) stage of intellectual development: (a) concrete operational; (b) formal operational; (c) preoperational; (d) sensorimotor.

15. A principal difference between concrete and formal operational thinking is: (a) a concrete operation is based on sensorimotor perceptions whereas a formal operation is based on logic; (b) a formal operation deals with logic whereas a concrete operation deals with preconcepts; (c) a formal operation deals with real events whereas a concrete operation is more symbolic; (d) concrete operations are tied to easily imagined events whereas formal operations are more symbolic.

16. A child is presented with thirty coins (some are pennies, some are nickels, some are dimes, and some are quarters). Next, the child is asked to name all the combinations that sum to exactly $1.03. The ( ) child will approach this task by directly testing a series of single predictions: (a) concrete operational; (b) formal operational; (c) preconceptual; (d) intuitive.

17. Which of the following terms does not belong to the adolescent? (a) idealism; (b) hypothetical thought; (c) formal operations; (d) intuitive thought.

18. ( ) is to the stage of concrete operations as ( ) is to the stage of formal operations: (a) Conservation; idealism; (b) Egocentricity; intuition; (c) Preconceptual thought; object permanance; (d) All of the above.

19. Which of the following statements is incorrect? (a) A delinquent is defined as a juvenile who has been apprehended and convicted for breaking a law; (b) Delinquency is more prevalent among boys than girls; (c) Lower-class children are twice as likely to commit delinquent acts as middle-class children; (d) There is a direct relationship between self-esteem and delinquency.

20. Which of the following statements is correct? (a) A child is more likely to become a delinquent if he or she belongs to a peer group that engages in delinquent behavior than if he or she does not belong to such a group; (b) Children from fatherless homes are less likely to be delinquent than those from homes with fathers, particularly if the father is permissive; (c) Due to recent changes in the definition of socioeconomic classes, the lower class is no longer significantly overrepresented in studies

185

of the incidence of delinquency; (d) All of the above are correct.

21. Which of the following statements is correct? (a) According to Lefrancois, most studies of drug use are probably overestimates of the nature of the drug problem; (b) The effects of smoking marijuana are highly predictable; (c) There is some evidence that LSD may produce changes in chromosomes; (d) All of the above are correct.

22. Recent research has shown that: (a) females are more likely to commit suicide than males; (b) smoking marijuana is highly correlated with suicide; (c) college students are more likely to commit suicide than non-college students; (d) all of the above.

Answers to Posttest

1. c (p.394) 2. a (p.395) 3. c (p.395) 4. a (p.395) 5. a (p.395)
6. c (p.397) 7. c (p.395) 8. c (p.401) 9. b (p.403) 10. a (p.408)
11. c (p.408) 12. d (p.409) 13. d (p.409) 14. b (p.412) 15. d (p.412)
16. a (p.412) 17. d (p.411) 18. a (p.411) 19. c (p.416) 20. a (p.416)
21. c (p.421) 22. c (p.422)